RENEWING TRADITION

THE ARCHITECTURE OF ERIC J. SMITH

RENEWING TRADITION

THE ARCHITECTURE OF ERIC J. SMITH

ERIC J. SMITH

FOREWORD BY ALEXA HAMPTON
INTRODUCTION BY MARISA BARTOLUCCI

RIZZOLI NEW YORK

New York · Paris · London · Milan

Foreword

by Alexa Hampton

As everyone knows, building, renovation and restoration can be hard work. It is messy. Invasive. Time-consuming. And expensive. It tests the patience of many and the very sanity of others. As someone who has literally grown up in this field, I have witnessed some truly odd events, and I have come to expect them as a matter of course during projects. Once, a planeload of overdue outdoor furniture was delivered to a client's house in the Bahamas, only to yield several tons of bananas that had been misdirected to us. Another time, scarier by far, a window was sucked out of an apartment building I was decorating — falling and shattering forty-four stories below, incredibly causing no damage or harm. I've installed a house in the Hamptons during Hurricane Irene and had to rebuild another after Katrina ravaged Louisiana.

Why do we keep building in the face of such trials? For the results: the creation of the perfect place to call one's own, imbued with one's own history and preferences, where balance, beauty and harmony seamlessly coexist. As Eric Smith says, the building of a legacy dwelling is the root of what we do, and Eric does just that very, very well. He is a brilliant architect with a pedigree to die for and a practice that spans the country, and decades. Logic and art are perfect partners in Eric's creative process. He is that rare architect whose approach is as practical and meticulous as it is informed and scholarly. He mines ideas modern and historic to create timeless houses that feel unstudied. More importantly, they feel inevitable. He encourages his clients to feel as well as to see the potential house, and therein lies just a small part of his genius.

During the many projects I have undertaken with Eric, he has been a generous listener and a nimble creative partner, always ready to think through variations while applying a relentless rigor to each iteration. Eric never refuses to consider an idea, but there is a twinkle that appears in his eye when one should, perhaps, give a matter a second thought. The result of that twinkle is what I call "The Eric Effect."

When I was working on my own apartment, which required the rejiggering of three small apartments into one, I had a tough time gracefully knitting them together. In all honesty, I spent an entire night awake, drawing and silently chanting "What would Eric do? What would Eric do?" My mantra yielded inspiration — I sketched something. That very week, I showed Eric my plan. He approved of it, but I saw that little twinkle. He gently explained how two closets I had drawn would just slightly pinch my family's new entrance hall, and he explained how this might diminish the experience of entering and the apartment's sense of welcome. He asked if I had considered deleting them. I was aghast. I told him, point blank, that a woman does not remove a closet, much less two, when a closet can be had. I felt his absence of double X chromosomes had really led him astray. Certainly, I was right on this. I was a grown woman, an experienced designer. He nodded his head, but the twinkle persisted. Two weeks later I deleted the closets. The entry is one of my favorite spaces in the apartment — he was absolutely correct. Voilà: the Eric effect.

Wonderful talent added to a wonderful temperament, a great sense of humor, and an "Aladdin's cave" of treasured knowledge is a rare combination — one that makes all the difference when striving to create beauty. Eric has a magic that he shares with his clients and his colleagues in his pursuit of excellence. He is completely dedicated to his work and it shows. And, I've never had bunches of bananas show up on an Eric Smith job site — *ever*.

An Enduring Legacy

by Marisa Bartolucci

It seems nothing short of providential that the first significant commission Eric J. Smith received as a newly licensed architect was the restoration of a David Adler-designed château in Lake Forest, Illinois. Just a few years out of school, and brimming with ambition, he was given the opportunity to study every detail of a fire-ravaged masterwork by one of America's greatest interpreters of classical European architecture and oversee its repair. The experience was not only a milestone for Smith — through the project's contractor he later met the classically minded, New York interior designer David Easton with whom he would collaborate for more than twenty years — but also something of a touchstone. Because if there is a true contemporary inheritor of the refreshed and bespoke classicism that David Adler's architectural practice exemplified, it is Eric J. Smith. And by working to uphold his legacy, Smith has become one of the most eminent classical architects of his generation.

For more than 30 years, Smith has designed, restored, and reshaped residences in various traditional vocabularies throughout this country as well as in Canada and in Europe. An active member in the Institute of Classical Architecture and Art (ICAA), he and his firm have been honored with the ICAA's prestigious Stanford White Award for Interior Architecture and Design for a stately stone Georgian that Smith built improbably — but with great technical brilliance, impressive craft, and an inspired appreciation for contemporary indoor/outdoor living — in California's Silicon Valley, a locale known for disruptions both cultural and seismic. You can read about its extraordinary making in these pages in the chapter entitled "California Georgian."

If you are unfamiliar with David Adler, you should know that the Milwaukee-born architect was in practice during the early decades of the twentieth century, designing most of his important residential projects in the environs of Chicago during the 1910s and 1920s. At a moment when modernism's pioneers were

conceiving radically novel and internationally oriented architectural expressions, Adler was making the case for how old-world forms could be re-imagined and scaled for the bold new American lives of that era's captains of industry. He promoted traditional vocabularies not so much out of an aversion for the new and universal, but out of a tremendous appreciation for craft, tradition, and locale.

Like Adler, who received his architectural training in Europe, Smith spent a formative college year abroad, studying architecture in Versailles and then making a grand tour of the continent's built masterworks. During these European sojourns, both practitioners gained fluency in the various architectural "languages" of the Old World, but never lost their American facility for — and appreciation of — contemporary invention. When Adler was called upon to design a "modern house" in the 1920s, he melded classical and modernist elements together with great panache to produce an entirely original residence. And as you can see here in the project entitled "Art Collector's Pied-à-Terre," when Smith was requested to transform an apartment in New York's downtown into a minimalist showpiece, he took that style's restricted architectural toolbox and with MacGyver-like ingenuity elegantly solved all kinds of tricky issues of space, light, and detail.

In short, versed as he is in traditional vocabularies, Smith designs eloquently in all architectural languages. It's revealing that he doesn't consider such an aptitude noteworthy. As he once remarked to me, "What determines whether a building is any good has nothing to do with its architectural clothing, but how good and solid its bones are." Which for Smith means a fine classic plan of light and view, framed by a structure with graceful lines and harmonious proportions. As you've no doubt surmised, the bones of all Smith's projects are always good and solid.

If Smith has continued in the tradition of Adler and other classicists from both the near and distant past, he is also very much a practitioner of his own making and times. I find it fascinating, for example, that Smith originally considered becoming a filmmaker; when he describes how he came to design a project, this early interest becomes apparent in the way he speaks of storytelling, visual pacing, and the angles by which the house or interior will be viewed. He habitually uses the phrase "buying time" when describing a project, an expression I originally took to mean the frequency with which he employed antique materials or artisan-made embellishments to endow a home with a sense of history; for him, however, the phrase encompasses much more than that. When he designs homes, Smith

actually tries to slow down the perception of time. He sites dwellings so you never see them along their axial line, only by an oblique view, heightening the anticipation of catching full sight of them, which, I think, adds to their allure. "Time really does seem to stand still in these homes," a colleague of Smith's once commented to me. "You feel so safe, like nothing bad could ever happen. That here you could be the best version of yourself." You certainly can't get more Old Hollywood than that!

Smith achieves the architectural equivalent of a perfected domesticity by considering long and hard how a home will be lived in, and what will be the experience of the residents moving about it and through its outlying buildings and grounds. How should an entry be framed so that a visitor will feel at once welcome and secure? Is there a way that the view of the bay beyond the house can become part of the initial threshold moment? Where should the tennis court be sited and how best to landscape around it, so it will enhance the view of the grounds when glimpsed from the house and not be an eyesore?

Over the years, Smith has become adept at envisioning whole projects from scratch — the building, the interior and its details, and the surrounding landscape design. He calls this approach "holistic design" and feels very strongly about the key role the architect plays in this overview. He's not alone in this conviction, of course, but other practitioners of his generation tend to talk in lofty terms about creating a Gesamtkunstwerk, "a total art work," which speaks, I think, about their professional self-importance. Smith is always keen to team up with interior designers and landscape architects at the start of a project who can contribute to and refine his vision; in fact, so collegial and creative are these collaborations that the same talents work with him regularly.

If a deeply ingrained humility sets Smith apart from many of his peers, it should be noted that what he lacks in vanity, he makes up for in self-assurance. This is an architect who radiates confidence. Speak to those who have worked with him — decorators, landscape architects, contractors, craftspeople, and clients — and they will tell you in almost reverential tones about how capable and knowledgeable he is. Words like "credibility," "authenticity," and "gravitas" are used. They marvel too at how passionate he is about his work, tracking the smallest details, but without micromanaging.

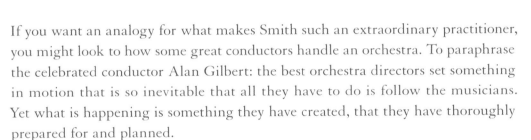

"Smith's belief in how essential a team of gifted tradespeople — from plumber to woodcarver — is to the making of a great building demonstrates a deep understanding of his profession's traditions."

As to the craftspeople and subcontractors on Smith's teams, I've been told they can be made uneasy by how conversant he is with the ins and outs of their trades. Yet once they've recovered from the shock of knowing that Smith has them in his laser focus, they often push themselves harder, showing off what they can do. Clients of Smith told me about how when their house was being built, the supervising carpenter once showed up at the crack of dawn, several hours before Smith was due to meet the team and review their progress. The carpenter had come early to rip out the bowed frame of the ceiling on the staircase. "It's about an eighth of an inch off. We could make it work, but Eric will know," he confessed to the couple, adding, "I'm inspired by his sense of precision, and I want to make this right."

If you want an analogy for what makes Smith such an extraordinary practitioner, you might look to how some great conductors handle an orchestra. To paraphrase the celebrated conductor Alan Gilbert: the best orchestra directors set something in motion that is so inevitable that all they have to do is follow the musicians. Yet what is happening is something they have created, that they have thoroughly prepared for and planned.

For Smith, a key element in the making of a successful project is the selection of the team: "Select the people who know how to build, how to problem solve, how to work collaboratively as opposed to independently or only being told what to do," he says. "Otherwise, if they weren't told the right thing, well, that's your problem, not theirs. You want people who will invest in the process. In most crafts, an artist invests in their process."

Smith's belief in how essential a team of gifted tradespeople — from plumber to woodcarver — is to the making of a great building demonstrates a deep understanding of his profession's traditions. It speaks to how imbued he is in classicism's notion of architectural expression as the mother of all arts, thoroughly fusing building science with aesthetics. This is why Smith still begins all of his design work by drawing; as his pencil races across a page in his sketchbook, clients can witness the rooms in their future home materialize before their eyes. And why he believes so fervently that custom-made detailing by experienced artisans, trained in crafts that have been used to fashion and adorn building for centuries, is essential to the construction of homes of enduring quality and value.

"That Smith reveres the idea of a house sheltering a family over the life cycle of several generations also speaks to his desire for tradition."

At the same time, it should be said that Smith is very much a twenty-first-century practitioner. His office is outfitted with the latest computers and architectural software. The traditional residences he envisions are purposely tailored to the modern needs and desires of those who will dwell in them. Indeed, Smith has told me that one of his greatest professional pleasures is deciphering his clients' domestic dreams and aspirations. It's one of the chief reasons he has concentrated his practice almost entirely on residential commissions. Is this again the filmmaker in him deciphering a character's motivations? Perhaps.

Yet his knack for developing easy intimacies with clients has to be one of his greatest standalone talents. Of course, he relishes all the technical aspects of his work, like the construction and the problem-solving. "It's all about finding complex solutions from the very first conversation you have with a client when they say: 'I have a vacant piece of land…' Or 'I've got this co-op…' Understanding the problem and how you might discover ways to unravel it is deeply satisfying," he says.

Once during a morning interview, Smith made a telling observation. He was soon to drive down to Princeton to supervise the finishing touches on a house he had designed there. His clients were scheduled to move in the following week. It was a bittersweet moment. "My role is almost over, other than being on call if the baby has a temperature," he said pensively. "It's now kind of turned over to the pediatrician who gets to be with the child for the next ten years; the decorators and the landscapers who will continue evolving their work after the client has moved in. But the midwife has moved on."

I've interviewed a lot of architects and I cannot think of a single one, women included, who would describe themselves as a midwife to a building. The right to claim some kind of parenthood, if not outright authorship of a home you've designed seems to go with the territory of being an architect, especially the principal of an acclaimed eponymous firm. But then again, Eric J. Smith isn't like most architects.

"... I suppose he's right to see himself as a midwife because he delivers beautiful homes born out of his clients' dreams. They certainly couldn't be in more talented, practiced, or safe hands."

When Smith was a boy, his own family moved around a lot due to his father's work; you don't have to be a Freudian to detect a longing for stability in his veneration of permanence and timelessness. That Smith reveres the idea of a house sheltering a family over the life cycle of several generations speaks to his desire for tradition. From various anecdotes of his, it's easy to glean that his favorite projects are those in which he's developed a rapport with the clients' children and has instructed them in the fundamentals of architecture and building. He's confided that watching these young people grow up in the houses he designed, while developing their own aesthetic sensibilities, has been deeply satisfying.

In fact, in another conversation, Smith pointed out to me that the word "client," derives from the Latin word *cliens*, meaning "one who is guided." That is "the role I think an architect should play," he mused. "One shouldn't impose one's will, ego, and whatnot on the process, but guide a client to understand and discover what they might want out of the project. And then guide them through the process in an experienced way to show them what can happen, and how things can work, and how to stretch their imagination." So at his core, Smith is as much a teacher — an instructor in the principles not only of design but also gracious living — as a gifted architect. By that measure, I suppose he's right to see himself as a midwife because he delivers beautiful homes born out of his clients' dreams. They certainly couldn't be in more talented, practiced or safe hands.

ST. GILES
ROYAL MILE
EDINBURGH
12·11·18

Buying Time, Telling Stories

by Eric J. Smith

When people find out that I am an architect, their first questions is usually "What style of work do you do?" My answer is often a variation of the theme that the best architecture that I know of is rooted in the classical. By this I don't mean necessarily the temples of Greece, or really any specific historic style that has evolved over the centuries, rather it is the classically inspired floor plan. The appeal of the traditional and symmetrical arrangement of spaces, inside and out, serves as the starting point for all the homes I design.

I found early on that I respond to older, classically inspired buildings created centuries ago, before there were the modern technologies of air conditioning, electric lights, glass windows or wood-stud construction. These designs by necessity provide good natural light and ventilation, to easily lead one through the spaces during the day and provide comfort and security at night.

There was the balance and symmetry of the spaces, the enfilade of one room following another on a direct line, naturally daylighting each with generous openings, windows placed to both light the way and to provide natural cross ventilation, often simply with shutters to close the space up when needed. The walls, inside and out, were thick, mass-bearing stone or brick, offering a sense of permanence and embrace. The roofs responded to the effects of the sun and rain or snow for each specific locale — deep eaves or porches for shade in the hotter or rainier climes, trimmed back in the cooler areas, steeply pitched in snowier areas — these buildings were designed to suit their sites. They were built, as we do today — for a specific purpose, by a particular client, on a unique site, responding to a specific geography and climate and have stood the test of time, some for centuries.

I believe classically inspired buildings speak to most people, even if only subconsciously. There is a clarity to the planning that makes it easy and stress-free to understand how one is to proceed through the spaces, a sense of comfort in the thickened walls and movement of air and light. Then there are the styles and details of the elevations that are overlaid on these plans to communicate the purpose of the building, the aesthetic of the client and architect, and the inherent history that these styles convey. Such buildings have served their purposes for generations.

Classically inspired buildings create comfort through the logic of their design, the inherent solidness of their construction, and the presence of detail that is familiar and enriching. These structures were built to last. And, in the homes we design for our clients, they still are. Entering these buildings, one experiences the fabric of history; by hewing to a classical vocabulary we evoke an earlier age in a way that slows down time, thus we are "buying" time.

Our homes share another common trait with older, classically inspired buildings: they tell a story. And it is in the stories that buildings tell, especially homes, that my story begins.

In looking back at the beautiful homes I have had the incredible good fortune to work on over these first thirty years of my practice, it's funny to think about how I ended up here — I actually did not set out to be an architect. Coming out of high school I wanted to be a filmmaker, to tell stories. It's why I enrolled at the University of Illinois Urbana–Champaign; at the time it had a good film program. But as fate would have it, no sooner had I arrived as a freshman than the university decided to revamp the art department and close the film school. It was a crazy time: I was a freshman starting college and I quickly had to rethink what I was going to do with myself. Should I stay at Illinois and choose another major, or transfer to another school with a film program?

If that wasn't a lot to handle, the university was also significantly overenrolled. That first semester there weren't enough dorm rooms, so I was assigned to a lounge where I had seven roommates. I wasn't very happy about being packed in like that, but in retrospect, it turned out to be an incredible opportunity. Such close quarters meant I was able to learn a lot about my roommates' intended majors: business, political science, engineering, and architecture. I soon focused on architecture because I saw parallels between making a film and making a building: both have a creative process and a production process, both have a tangible final product, and both tell stories. I still ask clients, "What story do you want your home to tell?"

Looking back, that fall semester freshman year was seminal for me even as the following years are something of a blur. As is true of most architectural programs, all-nighters become the norm and social life becomes a forgotten luxury. Happily, I excelled in my studies and for my senior year was accepted into the honors program at Versailles. Having the chance to go to France, to travel and study abroad profoundly changed my life. But before going any further, here is a little more background on me.

I'm the eldest of three children, born in Schenectady, New York. My father was a marketing executive with General Electric's air-conditioning division and my mom was a homemaker. Because of my father's job, we moved every two years or so to another GE town. By the time I graduated from college, we had lived in nine different homes, some in New England and in the Mid-Atlantic, and a few in the Midwest. All of that moving gave me a lot of experience with various kinds of houses, and by the time I went off to college I had opinions about how people should live in a home. I just didn't think these views would have anything to do with my career.

In those years I was the kind of kid who liked to build stuff in the backyard. Yet while I enjoyed constructing things, I never thought of it in terms of a profession. I liked to sketch too, especially boats. But when I was in eighth grade, my art teacher told me that I had no talent and should never take another art class. His rebuke so shocked me that I turned to photography and a number of years went by before I explored my creative side again.

"... there's nothing like sitting in front of a building and trying to draw it to really connect with it, to understand why it's there, how it interacts with light, how it fills space and how its details start to tell a story."

FRANCE
BEYNAC

In my senior year, I had one of those great teachers who are truly life-changing. I am sure we have all had them. I still feel indebted to Mr. Scharmann who taught Physics in Room 212. The issues probed by physics fascinated me: What's the force of gravity? How do things stand up? How do they move? That year, I also took an elective in mechanical drawing. I'm not sure they even teach it anymore. It was my first time using a straight edge, a T-square and triangle, drawing nuts and bolts and pieces of machinery. The whole experience gave me a lot of pleasure but, again, I didn't think it would have anything to do with my future. I already knew I would go into film; I had been totally captivated by a class on film and television my junior year and I saw film as a direct progression of years of doing photography. I was certain about my career in the way only teenagers can be sure of a life they have yet to live.

While physics and drafting had been fun — and ultimately relevant to my career — I was a clean slate when I joined the architecture program, which is why France and my travels in Europe were such an awakening. In class I had seen slide after slide of architectural masterworks, but that didn't prepare me for the experience of sitting in front of a building and trying to draw it; to really connect with it, to understand why it's there, how it interacts with light, how it fills space and how its details start to tell a story. In sketching there is always a best angle to show the building, and I found a natural connection to my earlier camera work. Where would I have set up the camera to capture what I wanted to show? It was an interesting continuum. And then, of course, there was the act of drawing itself.

There's nothing like the tactile connection of a pencil or a pen on paper to learn about something. Fortunately, I had taken a life drawing class before going to France, with a wonderful professor who mended the wounds of that eighth-grade art teacher. Each person in the class started by first drawing their thumb, then their hand, etc. The professor just built it up in a way that allowed all of us to see improvement — practice and more practice — the results were there in front of us. Drawing well is about having the confidence to put pencil to paper, and trust the process. With that teacher's help, I developed a new level of assurance that transferred to hard-line drawing and lettering classes (back then we were taught how to letter properly). All those classes were really meaningful to me. To this day sketching remains an essential part of the way I develop a design.

In France, the full-year program was a rotation of classes followed by independent study, during which I traveled from Copenhagen to Crete, sketching and drawing buildings and landscapes. It was on one such trip that I saw the Baths of Caracalla in Rome for the first time. Seeing it had a profound effect on me. I still find it an exciting space not just to look at, but to walk around and discover the views inside and out.

To my mind, it's essential to experience historical buildings in person. You can't get it from a book. It can start there, but you need to be in and around a building and its site: to see how people approach it, how they use it, how they interact and animate its spaces, how well the hallways and rooms allow people to navigate, its large or small scale. Only by experiencing a building, being in it, can one understand the stories it has to tell. Ultimately buildings have a purpose, they are virtually never simply objects: they are courthouses or schools or, in my case, homes.

During the summers I had my own business painting houses to earn money for college. The area of New Jersey where my parents lived had some beautiful old houses; I got to spend summers crawling all over those buildings and examining their architectural details. I especially remember burning years of paint off, scrutinizing some amazing moldings that had been made in the 1910s and 1920s. I learned a lot during those summers. It was then that an appreciation for historic architecture began to take hold.

The summer before my senior year, I served as an apprentice to Anthony Kovias, an architect with a small office: two desks, a phone, a coffee maker and an ammonia blueprint machine. I was right next to him, elbow to elbow. I got to see him do everything and be involved in everything, whether it was answering the phone, making blueprints, actually going out and measuring a site with him, or doing construction drawings. Mr. Kovias was a lovely man and very enthusiastic about me and my prospects. Interning for him turned out to be a beautiful entry into the profession, and I've tried to create a similar environment when I invite interns into our office. I haven't forgotten how impressionable and anxiety-ridden I was back then. So unlike some offices, rather than seating interns in the back and asking them to do the same thing again and again, I try to be as welcoming and supportive as I can be and to fully involve them in the range of work in the office. While I've experienced success in my career, at the same time I remember how nerve-wracking a profession architecture can be, especially at the beginning.

In 1979, after graduation, I went to work for a six-person firm in New Jersey, which, as the economy began to suffer, became a two-person firm, made up of the principal and me. As depressing as that must have been for him, it meant I had the opportunity to experience a lot of things I might otherwise not have had a chance to do. One project, in particular, turned out to be highly consequential — the restoration of a storefront that dated back to the early 1900s in the town of Red Bank. I researched the building and discovered that it had been "modernized" in the 1970s, covering all of its original detailing. I was able to uncover it, but many of the classical elements had been badly damaged, so I designed replacements. Quite unexpectedly the firm and I ended up winning an AIA award for the restoration — very exciting for a 23-year-old.

Not long after winning that award, the owner of the firm had to downsize to just himself. I wasn't sure what to do next, but two of my college classmates were living on the North Side of Chicago, so I moved there. Before long I was working at an architectural interiors office where I got to know one of the clients quite well. He owned a number of Holiday Inns; I did some work on them, which I considered dreadful. One day the client called and told me a fire had ruined

"The drawings, which I needed to restore the home, were not only relevant, they were invaluable. ...Their classical forms voiced a kind of timelessness that I found very meaningful. I saw that designing classical-style architecture was a way to 'buy time.'"

his house in Lake Forest — the whole attic had been destroyed and there was extensive water damage. He wondered if I would help him put it back together. It turned out that the house had been designed by David Adler, the master classicist who was responsible for designing some of the most significant residences in the suburbs of Chicago and elsewhere in the country in the 1920s and 1930s.

I jumped at the opportunity. I spent the next year on the project. I set up a satellite office for my firm in the house and researched all I could about it. At the Burnham Library at the Art Institute, I found some of the original drawings, actual blueprints from 1914, 1916 and 1920. I was struck not just by the beauty of the draftsmanship, but by how construction issues were solved by the detail and clarity of the drawings.

The drawings, which I needed to restore the home, were not just relevant — they were invaluable. They reminded me that the buildings I had studied in Europe — still being used today, hundreds of years later. Their classical forms voiced a kind of timelessness that I found very meaningful. I saw that designing classical-style architecture was a way to "buy time." In our homes, this happens through architectural detailing and the materials we use. Reclaiming old timbers or antique rooms, or buying a mature tree for the grounds of a house are ways to acquire history. By weaving old elements, antique or reclaimed, into a building, we evoke the ageless. With such elements, time seems to slow down. It is another way we "buy time" for our clients.

The contractor I worked with in Lake Forest was a true master builder; together we restored the house in a way that impressed the owner. Less than a year later, in 1983, just as I was passing my licensing exams, the contractor called to say he wanted to recommend me to a New York decorator he'd been working with, a traditionalist who needed a local architect to help him with a project that happened to be in Lake Forest. That's how I met interior designer David Easton.

Though twenty years my senior, David and I had an immediate connection. He had trained as an architect and had studied at Fontainebleau, and shared my enthusiasm for classical French architecture. Before starting his firm, he'd worked with Albert Hadley at Parish-Hadley, the legendary New York decorating firm, so he had a strong appreciation for decorated rooms with true architectural rigor. After the Lake Forest project was completed, David asked me to move to New York to work together on other projects and I readily agreed. Three years later I established my practice with his help. We continued to collaborate very closely and share office space for the next twenty-five years.

It's hard to express just how fortunate I was, as a still-young architect, to team up with David, who was both enormously talented and highly sought-after. Through him, I had the opportunity to contribute significantly to many extraordinary projects and learn even more about the intricacies of building, watching and talking with contractors, and getting hands-on experience in ways that simply aren't taught in school. I was able to collaborate with some of the world's greatest craftspeople and artisans, literally the best money could buy; they were some of my greatest teachers. I write more about them later in this book.

Many architects seek to impose their architectural vision. My experience in David's office was that we worked closely with our clients. They shared their dreams with us. We helped shape the vision. I still honor that stance; I have never felt it was my place to force my ideas onto clients. I believe when I'm hired to design a home, the clients trust me to realize the house of their dreams, not mine.

I think that architectural education too often overlooks the fact that clients commission buildings — clients are everything to a project. A client's tastes and desires are — like site and program — critical givens that I embrace as an architect. Throughout this book, I explain how intimately we work with our clients. It becomes clear that I consider many to be dear friends. As I learn each client's aspirations, habits and plans for the future, I know and understand them better, and can more helpfully interpret and clarify their desires.

Here our creativity and invention, our knowledge, experience and mastery all come together. I am able to sketch a room, a house or a landscape, to suggest its form and style, to give life and shape to the ideas that clients bring to us. When we are done we have created homes for our clients that honor their lives, their loves and their traditions. What follows are a few of my favorite homes.

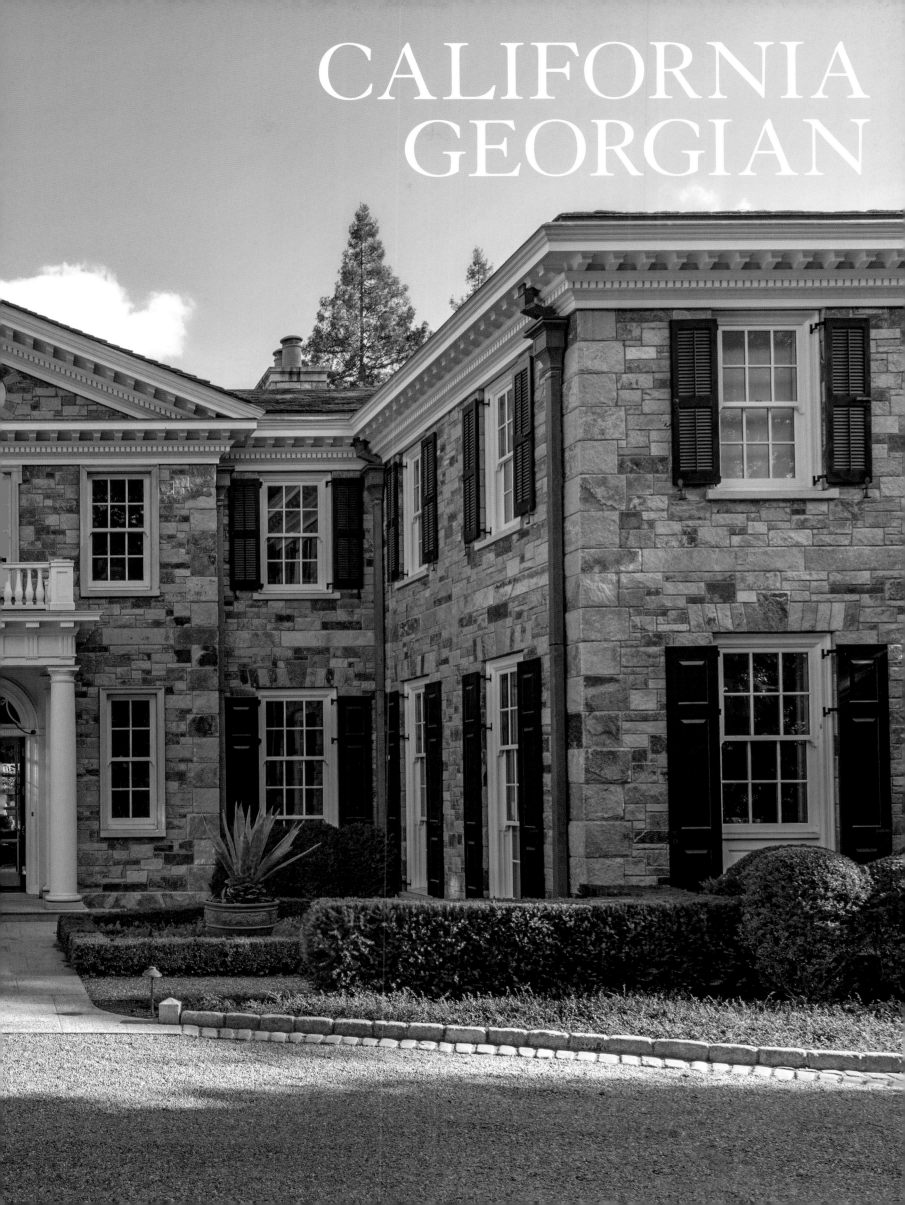

CALIFORNIA
GEORGIAN

RENEWING TRADITION

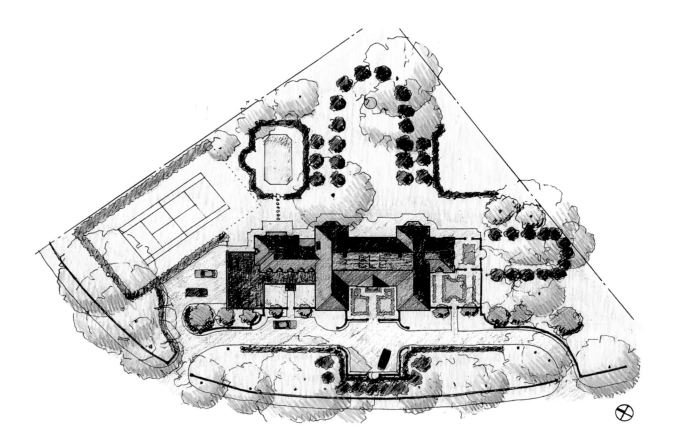

Creating a home that endures for generations involves a commitment of time and resources sufficiently substantial that it compels clients to take serious stock of what they value in their lives and how they wish to live. If they have children, they will consider the house as a supportive, nurturing framework for young lives, and then possibly again years later, when grown children have children of their own. It is not surprising, then, that creating a house, especially a legacy home, is always such an intensive process — it reflects our clients' dreams and aspirations.

The couple who commissioned this stone Georgian home in Northern California had moved eight times in the first seven years of their marriage, so they were already renovation and construction veterans. By the time I met them, they had been living in a Spanish Mission-style house in Silicon Valley for about a decade. The husband had accepted a position some distance away and with their eldest child happy at a school near his father's office, the couple decided to move closer to the office and school, with the hope that their three younger children would also attend in coming years. Instead of buying and renovating another house, they wanted to build one tailored to their tastes and desires.

What they had in mind was an elegant, permanent residence, one that felt as if it had always been there. They called Ed Lobrano, a decorator with whom they had previously worked, looking for an architect who could translate their ideas into a home. Ed had previously collaborated with me in the past and generously suggested our office. I flew out to California, and during our first conversation, I learned that they wanted a house with more of a traditional East Coast feeling and style, one that would convey a sense of timelessness. The husband is from Pennsylvania and the wife from Tennessee; they had met when in graduate school in New England and felt a deep connection to that area's classical-revival architecture. I first considered a Federal-style wood structure but thought instead that a stone Georgian was more in keeping with what we were discussing. Such houses, with their reassuring solidity and graceful proportions, offer a sense of permanence.

Opposite: Early in the planning it became clear that preserving several large and beautiful Heritage live oak trees was essential, and that the structure and driveway would have to be settled in and among them. The triangular lot was a particular challenge.

Above: The first site plan used the deepest portion of the corner lot to create the main axis and provided two driveway entries. In the final scheme we located the garage underground and omitted the tennis court, decisions that allowed us to maximize the property's sense of space.

While photos and books are helpful, there is no better way to discover if you like a particular style of architecture than to experience it in person. As it happened, I had worked on the design of a stone Georgian home in Connecticut not long before, and was able to arrange for the clients to visit when they were east for a family holiday. They were struck by the "feel" of the rooms, the balance and coherence of the plan, with one room leading naturally into the next. I remember too how impressed they were by the weathered look of the stone exterior, the living room's bow windows and the extensive gardens. Not long after this visit they commissioned me to design their new home.

The couple had purchased a triangular corner property with beautiful Heritage trees, including live oaks that were more than a century old and protected by local codes. The opportunity to place the house within that ancient stand was exactly the kind of setting I had hoped for, as it would support the sense of history a stone Georgian confers. Siting the house amidst these trees, though, was going to be a challenge. To maximize the amount of natural light the house would get we had to chart the path of the sun. And, because we would be excavating within feet of these Heritage trees, we had to carefully protect the root networks and, at the same time, ensure that these roots would not threaten the integrity of the foundation in the future. To accomplish this, expert arborists were hired to carefully hand-prune and burlap-wrap the roots. Once we had sited the house, we considered the arrangement of all the other elements that would be located on the grounds — a gracious drive, generous gardens, a formal swimming pool, and a four-car garage. We also conducted a thorough analysis of the geology within the buildable footprint.

Above: The principal view through the house to the rear yard starts from the entry court through the pair of front doors.

We soon learned that in addition to a high water table, just six feet below grade, the soil at the building site was largely expansive clay, a less-than-ideal ground material for a foundation. During the dry season, this type of clay poses few problems, but in the winter rains that so often affect northern California, it expands exponentially and can push a house right out of the ground. We would have to dig a twelve-foot-deep foundation to anchor the structure into the earth, and that created the opportunity to include a basement. A pivotal moment in the design occurred as we were considering the excavation and came up with a solution to free up more of the grounds: we would locate the garage below grade. This eliminated that sizable building from the site and increased the space for lawns, gardens and plantings. In my experience, every project that has challenges like these turn out to have unexpected opportunities.

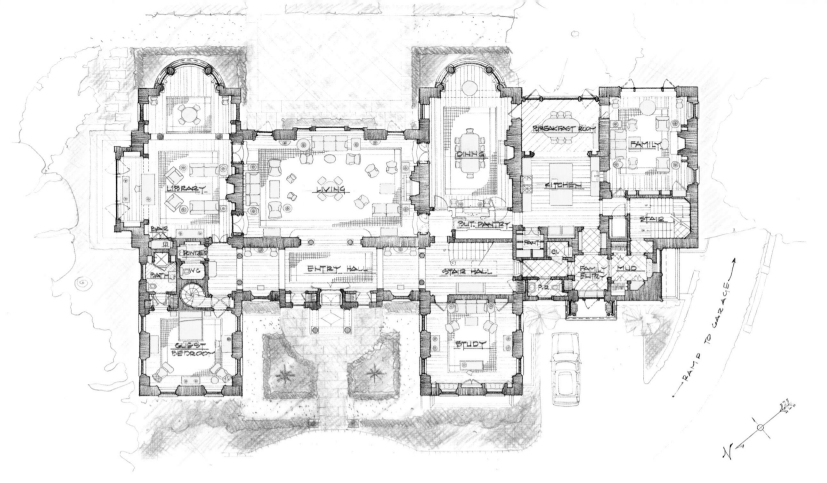

Building a two-story stone structure with a slate roof that complies with California's seismic codes was quite a task. In fact, at one point when the couple were at a cocktail party, they met a local architect and told him what they were planning to build, at which point he told them flatly: "It's not going to happen." It was difficult, but the skilled structural engineers we worked with accomplished the feat. Together we designed a seismic-absorbing steel framework that could be clad with a six-inch stone veneer to appear to be a solid stone house. In figuring out how to support this structure, connect it to the foundation, and counteract the hydrostatic pressure created by the high water table and type of ground material, our general contractor, Paul Ryan, was invaluable: we had to install a two-foot-thick concrete mat slab to serve as a sub-foundation, on which was placed a waterproof lining that wrapped all the way up to the exterior frame, like a pool liner.

This complex foundation, acting similar to the ballast in the hull of a boat, prevents the house from being uprooted no matter how much it rains. In the years since it was completed, the clients report the house has never experienced any uplift or, for that matter, any sway during an earthquake, or cracking of its foundation or walls: a testament to the know-how of our talented structural engineer and general contractor.

Early on, I introduced our client to Peter Cummin, the highly respected landscape architect with whom I have collaborated since 1984 and who had designed the landscape for the stone Georgian in Connecticut that had inspired my client. We marked out a private approach shielded from the street, a circular entry court with a central grassed mound (most cherished by the family's Irish Setters, who used it as an outlook), an aerial hedge, and the gravel drive continuing past the mudroom entry to the underground garage entry. Peter then plotted out the rear of the property, creating a sequence of garden spaces and woodland paths, including vegetable and cutting gardens. To focus this composition we designed a swimming pool flanked by olive trees, which is also part of the main axis that starts with the entry court and front door, and culminates with the semi-enclosed pool pavilion. That building and other outbuildings appear as if they had been built long ago, in service of the house. When the plantings were completed, we were captivated not only by their beauty but also by how aromatic they were. This sense has only increased over time as the plantings have matured. Peter and his team triumphed once again.

In researching this home's design we found inspiration not only in American period homes but also from the Georgian architecture of the United Kingdom and Ireland. These historic houses, with their graceful proportions and contrast of highly ornamental detail to clean and restrained lines, gave us a wonderful starting point.

Cutting stone in a previously abandoned Connecticut quarry with weathered fissures, and transporting it across the country was worth the effort, as the stone facade imparts a strong sense of history and permanence.

Left and above: The entrance establishes the main axis of the house — from the glazed front doors, through the entry hall, the generous central living room, and out to the pool and Poolhouse beyond.

Top: The cross axis of the front hall leads to the stair at one end, and a master guest suite at the other. The enfilade is naturally illuminated by the generously sized windows of the entry hall, living room and large main stair.

Above: In collaboration with our client, it was decided that there would be no curtains in the living room, or the rest of the house, allowing the architecture to be fully exposed. To accommodate privacy and control the amount of sunlight, we detailed motorized solar shades at each opening.

LIVING ROOM

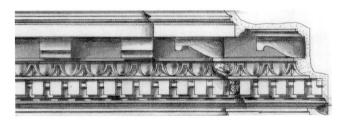

Top: My initial sketch for the living room.

Left: Detail drawings of the cornice moldings and door pediment, which were drawn at full size.

Following pages: The library, immediately off the living room and entry hall, is multifunctional, also serving as an office and a media room with concealed projector and drop-down screen.

We used Nordic pine, one of my favorite woods, in the library, as it best resembles the first-growth American white pine found in many early homes. Its light tone doesn't feel dark or heavy, rather, it adds a cozy warmth to the space and speaks to an earlier period and lifestyle.

While the house is framed in steel, it looks like a solid stone home. How does it so convincingly resemble an old masonry structure? One of the most important things we did was to find a source for the right stone to give the house a weathered, aged look. Obtaining "old" stone can be far more difficult than locating reclaimed wood or even antique parquet. We were fortunate in that when we built the stone house in Connecticut we had discovered a granite quarry that had once provided the stone for the Brooklyn Bridge but had been closed for some time. I was again able to select aged-face granite that had been exposed to rain and wind over many years, which we cut from the quarry's deep fissures, being careful to protect their weathered surfaces. At the quarry, the purveyor set up a cutting station to fashion the fieldstones, arches and quoins. For the latter, this process involved "pistol cutting" each piece of stone into an L-shape that could be affixed to the frame wrapping the corners of the house, making it appear to be solid stone. Inside the house, we designed deep-paneled reveals around the doors and windows, and between the rooms to further give the impression of thick bearing walls; we then used these generous interstitial spaces to locate the HVAC, electrical, and plumbing systems, as well as hidden storage.

Though the house looks as if it has been there for more than a century, it is outfitted with the latest technologies, all meticulously concealed. The house is so convincing in its appearance that just after the stone facade had been completed, a neighbor walking by asked how the "renovation" was going. The house appeared so at one with the site, he had forgotten that it was new!

These pages: The paneling and cabinetry we designed for this library were built and installed by Charles Manners, a master cabinetmaker based in England. All of the woodwork was shipped to California for Charles and his crew to install.

Interior doors are crotch veneer mahogany; wood floors are wide-plank, aged English brown oak. Both were hand-finished to create a patina that reinforces an overall sense of age in the home.

DINING ROOM.

After so many adventures in renovating houses, the wife had become a confident decorator and chose to handle the interiors herself, relying on us to serve as a sounding board and help her with contacts and sources. For example, we introduced her to a textile designer, Dennis Lee, to aid in developing the design of rugs for the living room and dining room, which are based on an antique Portuguese needlepoint rug she had once admired in a museum. We also helped her realize her idea for the wallpaper in the formal dining room. Looking at illustrations from her young children's plasticized placemats depicting native bird species in northern California, she thought to translate that idea into wall covering. We connected her with Gracie, a studio in New York that specializes in hand-painted custom wallpaper. They substituted the native birds and plants depicted for the flora and fauna in one of their traditional chinoiserie designs.

Charles Manners, who is also a highly skilled furniture restorer and fabricator, copied a pair of antique chairs the clients owned to create a set of 12 dining chairs.

Opposite: One enters the dining room through the living room using a centrally located portal, framed by a pair of Harmon-hinged mahogany doors, that focuses the view on the antique dining room mantle surrounded by Gracie wallpaper.

Above: My initial sketch for the dining room.

Above: Antique dining room mantle surrounded by Gracie wallpaper.

Opposite: The semicircular, full-height bay window, flanked by triple-hung windows at the east end of the dining room is set apart by a paneled jamb and beam. In plan, this is symmetrical with the bay in the library. In combination, these bring in significant natural light and dramatically frame the views to the rear garden and dining terrace. The table in this bay provides an intimate dining experience for groups of four to six people, impossible in the larger portion of the room.

As with many families, the kitchen of this house is the center of activity. To enhance that, we extended the kitchen with a forged-steel-and-glass conservatory to provide space as a breakfast porch and informal dining area. The glass roof enhances the sense of this space having been "added," and provides significant daylighting well into the kitchen. Even on the grayest of winter days, the kitchen glows with bright daylight from the glazed roof and offers expansive views onto the rear lawn and garden.

The oak plank flooring that we used elsewhere on the first floor is continued into the kitchen and family room. The flooring transitions to limestone in the conservatory, and an "exterior" wall of the stone house is "exposed" on one side, reinforcing the sense of its having been added at a later date.

The Georgian Gothic detailing, introduced in the dining room, continues through the cabinetry in this room, including the colonnettes that frame the opening of the conservatory. These are actually functional, as they open up to reveal storage for spices, cooking supplies, et cetera.

Top left: The butler's pantry features a traditional mahogany countertop, decorative glass-fronted cabinets.

Left and following pages: The kitchen opens through an oculus portal to the family room beyond, providing a connection with the family as they're relaxing and watching television. The kitchen also serves as a "pivot point," allowing easy movement between the butler's pantry, dining area, and mud room.

With an eye to the future, when the client may choose to live on the first floor, we designed a large master guest suite at the opposite end of the home from the kitchen. This room features a combination of double- and triple-hung-windows on three exposures. The decision here, as in the rest of the house, to not use curtains creates a stronger connection with the outdoors, and reveals the architectural detail. Thickened window jambs reinforce the sense of a true masonry home.

Filling out the first floor is the chinoiserie-inspired powder room, which accommodates guests and family at the library end of the home.

The main stair is daylit by a Palladian window on the landing between the two floors. Through the window, one can see a magnificent redwood, one of the Heritage trees around which we designed the house.

Above and left: The first floor includes a master guest suite, intended for visiting friends and older parents; it is also large enough to become the master bedroom in the future. Generous fenestration, including triple-hung windows, fills the room with soft, natural daylight year-round.

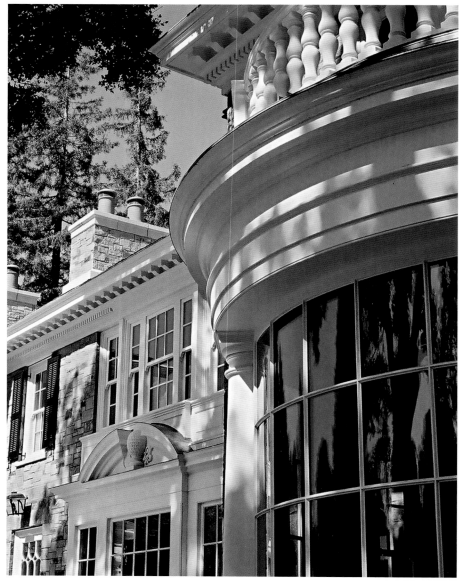

Above: The family enjoys entertaining and dining on the main terraces and its two small adjacent knot gardens. Landscape architect Peter Cummin stunningly integrated the gardens into the site with a focus on the pool and Poolhouse. A garden path meanders through the perimeter trees and planted woodland gardens, in contrast with the more formal gardens nearer the house.

Opposite: Looking back from the Poolhouse, we especially love the now-mature olive trees on either side framing the view.

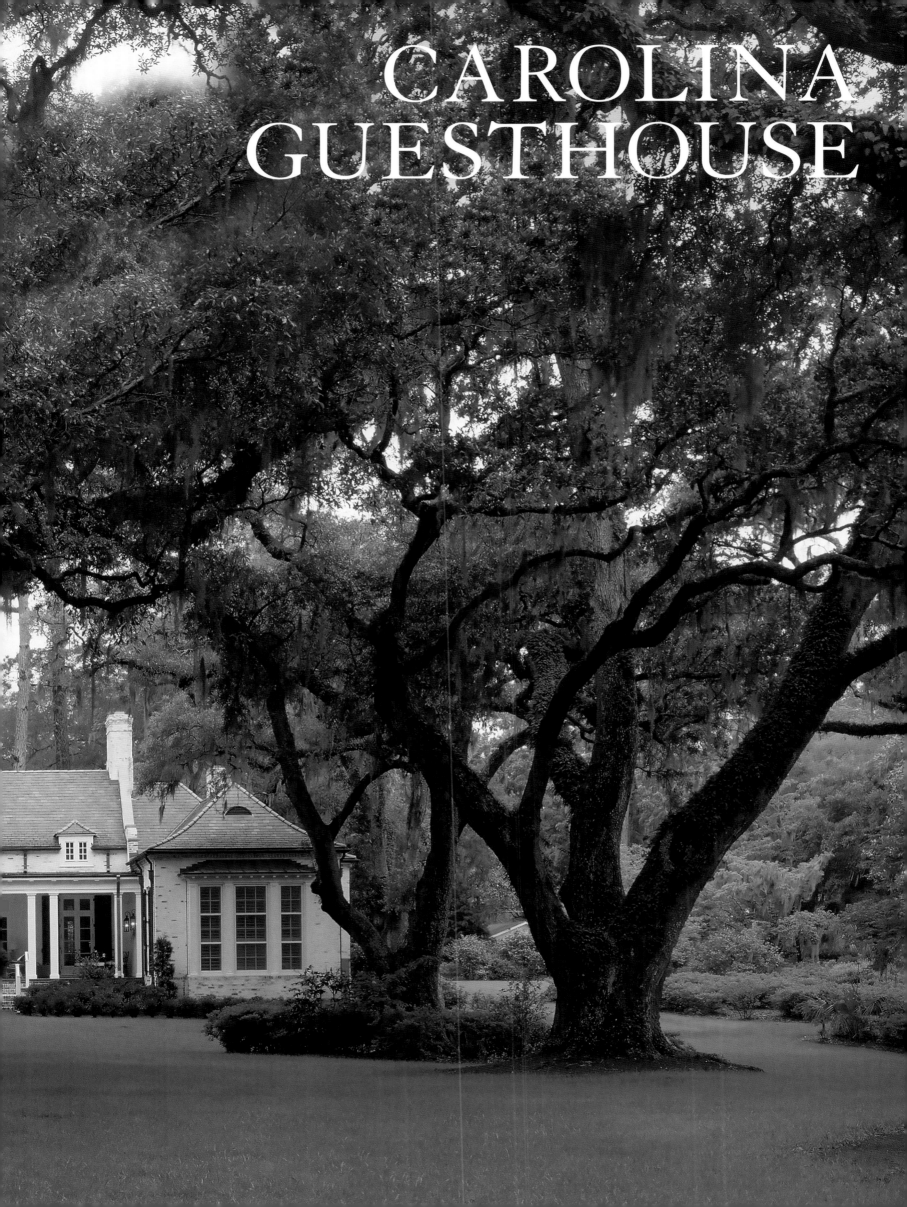

CAROLINA
GUESTHOUSE

With its H-shaped footprint, this guest cottage offers generous windows in every room, bringing in as much natural light as possible.

Local craftspeople rendered the roof by hand; with a gently curving profile, the roofline reinforces the impression that the building dates to an earlier time.

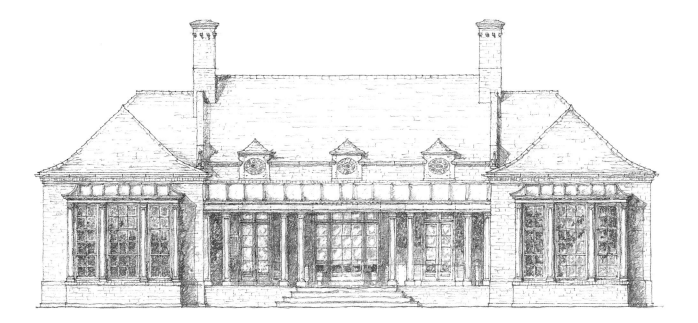

Gracious, yet petite, this house serves as guest accommodations for a plantation near Beaufort, South Carolina. In the late 1930s, the property, which encompasses more than seven miles of riverfront and marshland along with an extensive stand of timber, was purchased by a midwestern retail and publishing tycoon who was an avid sportsman. He and a close friend, also a publisher, loved this property, where they could hunt, ride and fish with their families from late fall to early spring. The original Civil War–era house had been destroyed in a fire, so at the end of a long allée of live oaks dripping with Spanish moss, these owners built a classic six-bedroom, whitewashed brick manor house, with an elegant slate roof set amid ryegrass lawns, azaleas, camellias and other flowering trees and shrubs.

Over the years, the plantation became so beloved by the families that the next generation decided to build a three-bedroom Guesthouse to host additional family and friends. It was critical that the new building be in keeping with the style and feeling of the existing house and grounds; they wanted it to look as if it too had been built nearly a century or so before. When a member of one of the families asked their friend and decorator, Anne Geddes, to refer an architect for the project, she very kindly suggested me.

Siting was essential to creating the illusion that the Guesthouse had always been part of the grounds. A logical spot presented itself at the end of the allée of ancient live oaks on the cross axis of the Main House; it now frames the Guesthouse and offers an enchanting view of the marshlands to the south and a mature camellia garden to the north. When conceiving the design, we had the extreme luxury of not being distracted by needing a driveway or parking; cars are kept elsewhere so as not to disturb the tranquility of this truly serene place. The owners, their guests, hunting parties, and staff travel around the grounds by foot, bike, or electric ATV.

In considering the program for the guest cottage, I learned — and was very influenced by — the rituals of shooting. The days start before daybreak, when a guide takes parties out to different parts of the property for a morning of shooting. Sometimes returning at midday, the hunters spend the next few hours lunching and relaxing before setting out again just prior to dusk. In the early evening they wash and dress for dinner, joining their hosts at the Main House, where, in the formal dining room, they recount the adventures of the day.

Following pages: Resawn trusses and loblolly pine flooring milled from the plantation's trees contrast with whitewashed oak plank walls, softly upholstered chairs and sofas, colorful fabrics, and delicate antique wall sconces.

To support these enduring traditions, the Guesthouse required an ample mudroom where hunters can stash boots, waders and guns after the hunt so that staff can clean and prepare everything for the next outing. It was also important to include a small but functional kitchen for breakfast and midday meals, and a warm and convivial gathering place, a common room, for afternoon reading and card games.

As she already knew what the owners liked in a country house, Anne decorated the bookcase-lined living room with Oriental rugs, dark wood furniture and overstuffed sofas to make a familiar, easy retreat. The main bedroom is done in a blue-and-white palette with French provincial prints, and the two smaller bedrooms have similar styles. Anne gave the rooms a sense of elegance and comfort.

As dinners are served in the Main House and lunches are sometimes taken during hunting outings, it made sense to design an abbreviated kitchen in the cottage, where guests can make coffee and breakfast, as well as light meals. A fully furnished bar extends the sense of Southern hospitality.

Most mornings are balmy enough to enjoy breakfast on the porch, which affords a view of the Main House as well as the stunning, historic allée of live oaks.

I knew that I wanted wood flooring for most of the Guesthouse, but it was only after a drive around the property with the plantation manager that we came up with the idea of using timber from the plantation for the Guesthouse's wood floors. The plantation regularly harvests lumber, so I chose some loblolly pine that had been felled the previous year and the contractor sent it to a local sawyer who cut it into wide planks.

Taking cues from the Main House, we built the Guesthouse with whitewashed brick and used slate for the roof. Unlike the Main House, the Guesthouse has a generous porch for sitting, reading or taking daytime meals. We also outfitted every exposure with shutter-trimmed, triple-hung windows, our own take on Low Country vernacular. We updated tradition in other discreet ways. The clerestory dormers we inserted not only filter daylight into the vaulted common room but give a sense that at one time the building had contained a second story; this hint of a possible past history enhances the cottage's aura of age and service. Together the spacious common-room ceiling, French doors and clerestory dormers ensure that even during the short days of winter it is a luminous space.

As disruptive as stripping a house down to its studs can be — in this case, the owners had to move out for nearly two years — it is also illuminating, as it reveals all of a house's mysteries and previous repairs so that intelligent changes can be made to improve its livability and lifespan. The owners and I took full advantage of this opportunity to re-envision nearly the entire home. Beginning at the front door, we replaced the solid door with one that had glass panes, immediately offering views through to the Sound — even from the road. Next was the main stair; before the renovation, guests entering the home looked directly up a flight of stairs into a second-floor bedroom. To craft a more gracious transition I reversed the staircase, allowing visitors to enter more formally, via a foyer with the focus now on a wider view of the living room and the water beyond. The new stairway descends to the living room side, which makes more sense aesthetically and functionally. As the stairs gracefully wind up and around the foyer, we added a luminous, book-lined window seat on the landing.

We then looked at the rest of the first floor and replanned the location of the library, living room and family room, and in the process created a much-needed study for the wife. In the new living room, we added a large box bay window opposite the entry door to anchor the seating arrangement and frame that dramatic water view. Not surprisingly, that room is the family's favorite.

Opposite: The importance of the main axis, from the front door through the house and to the Sound, is paramount. Adding glass to the front door extends this axis, accentuating this long view.

Top and middle: Black-and-white photos show "before" and "during."

Bottom: Re-imagining the entrance sequence amid a complete gutting of all but the shell. I still remember standing in the basement and seeing all the way up to the underside of the roof.

To further strengthen the indoor/outdoor connection of the house, we added deep porches along the back of the house facing the water. These spaces became outdoor living rooms, as they are contiguous with the living room, library and kitchen. Being able to sit outside in summer in the protected breakfast area or off the library when it rains are special pleasures. The new porches contribute to a wonderful plan, not just on the first floor, but on the reimagined second floor.

ENTRY HALL

Opposite: The new double-height entry is awash in light from the glazed front door and arched window at the landing.

Top: My original sketch from the front entry, reversing the stair.

Left: The doorway to the living room and the new box bay dramatically frame the view of the sound, creating a memorable entry experience.

Above: Original entry with its low ceiling and front door-facing staircase.

LIVING ROOM

Above: My initial sketch for the living room included a new fireplace. The design was modified to create space for a baby grand piano and bar banquette.

Right: In the living room, we extended the space with a box bay of full height glass, expanding the view to the water. The mirrored door on the left leads to the kitchen; it is balanced by a false door on the right for symmetry.

The Nordic pine–paneled library at the south end of the house connects to both the living room and the wife's study, which provides for a circular flow of traffic, important every day and for gracious entertaining. The library also opens up onto an exterior porch that extends the room and serves as an outdoor living room in the summer.

Previous pages: View from the entry through the living room to Long Island Sound.

Above: The wife's study includes a work area, concealed storage, and powder room. The walls were painted an unusually deep persimmon color that is quite bold and very uplifting.

This room is both a dedicated work space and a connection from the entry hall through to the new library.

Opposite: The library, with its Nordic pine–paneling and large fireplace, has direct access to the covered porch, which is used as an outdoor living room.

The windows flanking the fireplace were both widened and elongated, and we provided recessed pockets for the curtains so that the architecture can be more easily seen and expressed. These windows offer a view onto a small pond and gardens in the side yard.

For the gardens I recommended the landscape architect Peter Cummin, who helped reconfigure the front and side yards, as well as the garden on the southwest side of the house. Working with the wife, a skilled and knowledgeable gardener, Peter chose dense, richly textured shrubs along the lot lines on both sides, and plantings that bloom in three seasons in the gardens and borders. We worked together designing sitting areas, trellised paths and an outdoor dining patio, and conceived a new exterior lighting scheme, welcoming visitors in the evening.

LIBRARY

Above: With only two people living in the house much of the time, the kitchen is quite compact; the cooking area is contained on a short wall and separated from the breakfast room by an eat-in counter.

Right: The breakfast room, which is contiguous to the kitchen and family room, looks onto spectacular vistas of Long Island Sound and opens to a covered breakfast porch.

Cerused oak is used as a complement to the pine library at the opposite end of the house and creates a warm, cozy space for the family.

Opposite: View from main stair landing.

Above: The new staircase features an alcove with a built-in window seat nestled into the landing — a charming space for sitting, daydreaming or reading. The arched window relates to the curving stair wall and brings even more light into the hallways and stair.

RENEWING TRADITION

MASTER BEDROOM

The clients had embarked on the renovation both to improve the house as a weekend retreat and as a gathering place for their extended family. Thinking about this kind of multi-generational living, we created a master suite at one end of the second floor, with his-and-her dressing rooms and bathrooms, accessed by a short hall for privacy. All the guest bedrooms were reworked to create en-suite baths. The previously separate caretaker's apartment above the garage was transformed into a generous, family-sized guest suite, and is now connected to the rest of the second floor by a new exercise room with great views. Above the new first-floor porches, we created private decks outside the master suite, husband's study, and main guest bedroom. To visually unite these outdoor spaces, we designed a Chippendale-style railing, giving the house a more cohesive rear facade.

My goal with this home was to reenvision how it could be lived in by one, two, or even three generations at the same time. This vision was complemented by working closely with David's office, especially José Carlino, who, having worked on the clients city apartment were able to re-purpose much of the couple's original furniture, only reupholstering a few pieces, then creating a calm color palette for most of the house, to be counterpointed by the strong colors of her study and the dining room. For this nearly century-old home, we managed to preserve or rebuild the best of the old with the subtlest, most relevant, and best aspects of the new.

My redesign of the upstairs was driven, in large part, by a desire to "insulate" the master bedroom and make it more private. It is now separated from the main hallway by two sets of double doors and a small hall that accesses dressing rooms and bathrooms on the way to the master bedroom.

Above: The sketch for the master bedroom.

Above and opposite: Long Island Sound is visible from the husband's dressing room and bath. The gray and white palette, including Calacatta marble, brings warmth to these spaces.

Following pages: The new master bedroom with tray ceiling, generous doors and windows to a new deck and views of the water.

These pages: New porches were extended along the entire length of the house. The owners enjoy the stunning views of the Sound at the edge of the lawn and the ease of living outdoors when the weather allows.

FLORIDA
RIVERFRONT

This project in Jacksonville, Florida, actually started years earlier in Greenwich, Connecticut. It was there that I designed the renovation of a home for a busy family of four: a business-executive father, one child in college and one finishing high school, and a mother recently returned to university to study theology. Upon retirement and after enjoying many years in that home, the parents moved to Jacksonville, where the wife had grown up. Soon we were working together on the renovation of their new retirement home on the St. John's River. Shortly afterward, their grown daughter, now a pediatrician, moved nearby with her husband and two sets of young twins and commissioned us to design their new home. I had developed a real friendship with the parents when we did that first house in Greenwich, and even more so during our recent work together. Being able to work with the next generation of this family was especially rewarding.

The property the younger couple acquired was, in fact, the house the daughter's mother had grown up in, her grandparents' home, the site of many cherished childhood memories. It was a narrow but pretty lot with a fifties—era ranch house fronting the river, and long views of downtown Jacksonville some six miles across the water. The modest house had endured decades of Florida weather, including numerous tropical storms and hurricanes. It also lay perilously low on the land in an area prone to flooding. From an architectural and structural standpoint, restoring and adding to the existing structure to create a home for a family of six didn't make much sense, yet the prospect of tearing down the home was very emotional.

Understanding our client's deep attachment, we discussed what about the house — physically — was especially meaningful to her. She told me how much she loved the placement of the kitchen sink, the breakfast table, the fireplace (this is northern Florida, so it does get chilly in winter), and the view from her grandparents' bedroom. When she and her husband explained what else they were looking for in a house, I started sketching. Fairly quickly we developed a design for a northeastern coastal—inspired, shingle-sided house with a kitchen sink, breakfast table, fireplace, and bedroom situated just about as they were in the grandparents' house.

Our design for the new, two-story residence would have an H-shaped floor plan to maximize light and exposures, and a porch across the back to serve as an east-facing outdoor living room. Shaded and offering a nice breeze and beautiful views across the water, this porch is a lovely space for the family to enjoy the outdoors from morning till night. As the lot was narrow with neighbors close on each side, we conceived the house's main axis to be front-to-back, creating a sense of transparency by emphasizing the view to the water that starts at the front door. Knowing they would soon have a lovelier new home that honored her grandparents' house, she agreed to move forward.

With a basic plan and sketch elevation in hand we set about to flesh out a design that would feel as if it had been there for some time, with a strong architectural vocabulary that could be lived in and well used. Our design included large hurricane-rated windows that would provide ample natural light, greater access to views, and survive the on-shore storms this house was built to endure. Traditional detailing and quality materials on the interior and exterior would be "original," but updated, something that was important to everyone.

One of the ways that we reinforced the sense of age on the interior was to use reclaimed oak for the flooring. I'd found some wonderfully patinated planks from a two-centuries-old tobacco barn in northwestern Connecticut. Not only did the couple agree to use it, but the husband took on the role of "antique flooring purveyor" and coordinated the entire flooring order directly from the seller.

Opposite, top: Early design studies are very close to the final house.

Opposite, bottom: Faded shingles with black shutters, a pair of brick chimneys, sloping rooflines, almost perfect symmetry and a traditional architectural vocabulary bring more than a bit of New England style to this Florida house.

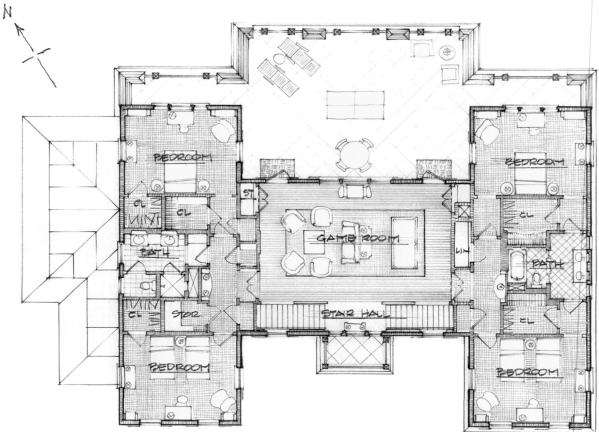

Second Floor

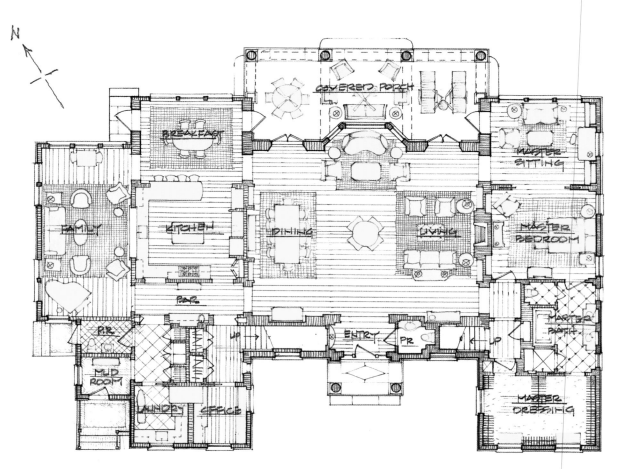

Previous pages: On-axis from the front entry, the main living/dining area offers a generous riverfront view. A central seating bay helps establish a feeling of space, orderliness and welcome. The living and dining areas are designed to flow into one another or to be divided as needed when guests are meeting, eating or visiting, all of which happen frequently.

Above: First- and second-floor plans. As with all of our designs, furniture is always drawn in to show scale, function, and circulation of the spaces.

Right: The living room features a hand-carved wood mantel, built-in bookshelves and cabinetry.

First Floor

Not surprisingly, given the mother's pastoral career, the couple are active in their church and community. Being able to easily entertain often and for many different kinds of occasions was very important; they wanted the ability to gather informally in several seating groups but to also seat up to fifty for dinner. That request became central to the planning as we worked out the flow between the living room, kitchen, family room, breakfast room, and porch, opting to omit a separate, formal dining room. The result is an open main room, with separate living and dining areas bisected by the axis established by the entry door on the land side and a large bay window opposite, overlooking the water. Painted ceiling beams subtly reinforce the division of space. This arrangement makes for a beautiful and flexible series of spaces where family and guests can join each other in small-scale gatherings, large sit-down dinners, or anything in-between.

Thinking about the distant future as well as the present, I suggested locating the master suite on the first floor, with the children upstairs. It seemed odd at first to the clients as they were so young, but there was a moment during the design phase when, as they became more enthusiastic about the suggestion, I recall the wife laughingly telling me: "The only way I'm going to go out of this house is feet first!" The master suite is gracious, with a bedroom, bath, dressing room, and sitting area that doubles as an office from which a large pair of pocket doors can be opened or closed to separate this space from the bedroom. One pair of French doors lead out onto the porch overlooking the water and another back to the living room, reinforcing the continuous circulation of the plan.

Top: The master bath links the master bedroom to the dressing room, which also opens out to the porch, allowing husband or wife to leave the master suite without disturbing their sleeping partner.

Right: The master bedroom can be closed off from the sitting room via generous full-height pocket doors. The sitting room, which doubles as a small office, is connected to the porch and living room by French doors.

The couple wanted the children to have bedrooms of their own, but they felt each set of twins should share a bathroom. They considered it to be good training for when the kids left home. The second-floor plan locates the children's bedrooms at the four ends of the "H," each with three exposures. My idea that the four bedrooms would connect to a central upstairs game room, one that could later be converted into a teen hangout, was endorsed enthusiastically. Wise parents, they liked the idea that their teenage children would be within earshot when they were all at home, rather than in a separate wing or above the garage. We designed an ample common space adjacent to the four children's bedrooms. As the climate is nice for most of the year we took advantage of the roof over the first-floor porch to create a very large second-floor deck where everyone can enjoy outdoor space to read, sunbathe, play ping-pong or just be outside — and the view isn't bad either!

Opposite: The game room is centrally located on the second floor between the four children's upstairs bedrooms. Filled with overstuffed chairs and sofas, it is grown-up enough to host any of the family as well as teenage friends. A large deck facing the river is just outside.

Above: Each of the four children has their own bedroom, with an extra bed so a sibling or friend can easily sleep over.

Accessed from the living room, breakfast and master sitting areas, this centrally located porch underscores the ease of living in Florida, where indoor-outdoor space makes sense much of the year. Being able to sit on a shaded porch and look out onto the water instills a deep sense of tranquility and connectedness to the landscape.

Our goal was to combine a traditional aesthetic with great pragmatism in just about every aspect of this house, starting with the preparation of the land with a stabilizing practice called "loading the site." Once the old house was removed and before we began construction, we reinforced the bearing capacity of the existing soil by loading three feet of clean soil on top of the existing ground level, over an area slightly larger than the building's footprint. Over the course of a year, an engineer monitored the soil as it self-compacted until it was adequate to bear the weight of a two-story house. In addition, at the husband's suggestion, we raised the first floor of the house an additional eighteen inches, going beyond code mandate. This proved to be prophetic when Hurricane Irma pounded Florida in 2017, inundating Jacksonville with flooding not seen before. The first floor of the house was still a full foot above the floodwaters.

The home has served the family well. The children are now either out of college or soon to be so. The couple are enjoying their empty nest, knowing that of their chicks will always have a place to come home to, just down the road from their grandparents, with whom this project started all those years ago!

Left and following pages: The house, as well as the land, has been raised eighteen inches above code to make it even less susceptible to storm-related flooding. The outdoor living spaces are connected across the back of the house: the master sitting at one end; the breakfast room at the other; and the living room in the middle.

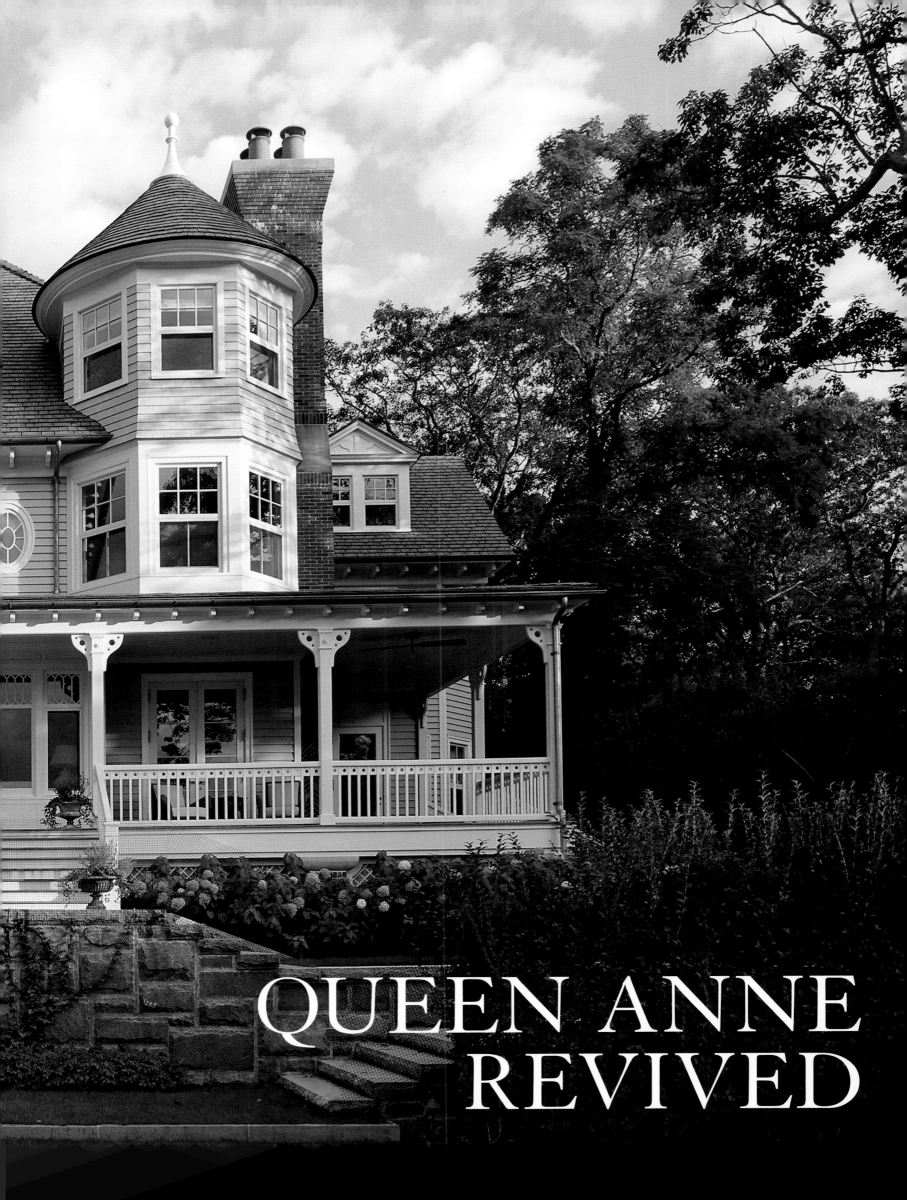

QUEEN ANNE
REVIVED

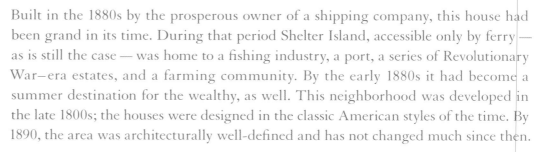

These pages: The house before the renovation.

Top: The east elevation with a basement-level entrance, formerly the back entrance; later it became the de facto front entry. You can see the old fire escape ladder on the back facade.

Middle: The existing front door, when we first visited the site.

Bottom: The original porch.

Built in the 1880s by the prosperous owner of a shipping company, this house had been grand in its time. During that period Shelter Island, accessible only by ferry — as is still the case — was home to a fishing industry, a port, a series of Revolutionary War–era estates, and a farming community. By the early 1880s it had become a summer destination for the wealthy, as well. This neighborhood was developed in the late 1800s; the houses were designed in the classic American styles of the time. By 1890, the area was architecturally well-defined and has not changed much since then.

In the shipping owner's day, visitors were transported from the ferry to their lodgings by horse and carriage. For this home, they would be delivered to its west side, where they would climb the steps up the hill and onto the porch; turning around they would find a stunning view of the bay. Meanwhile the carriage would continue on with the luggage to the servants' entry at the rear of the house. Those taking care of the luggage would enter at ground level, which was actually a partial basement that included a staff room, stair and, more importantly, the kitchen. The trunks would then be hoisted up the stairwell to the attic trunk room — the hook for this was still in place when we started.

Sometime during the Second World War or shortly after, the rear of the house became the front; as its owners were now living with less staff and driving their own car, which they parked nearby in the old carriage house. It was an inevitable switch. Unfortunately, this side of the house was not as handsome and entering at the basement level was neither well-organized nor gracious.

Our clients are a family who summered for several years in a quirky Victorian nearby. It was only when they were expecting their fourth child that they finally decided to put down roots here, which is how they came to acquire this sprawling house high on a bluff with superb water views.

It would be entirely fair and true to say that the house, when we first saw it, had a lot of "issues." For any new owner, the entry via the basement was entirely unacceptable; it was awkward and simply impractical. Similarly, the floor plans, typical of the Victorian era, featured small parlors on the first floor and upstairs bedrooms that shared a hall bath. On each level, the windows weren't at all attuned to the vistas beyond. The kitchen, as noted, was still in the dank basement; the main stairs and principal chimney mass blocked the views to the water from the main rooms; and there was very little connection to or interaction with the exterior living spaces — either to the porch or the sloping grounds surrounding the home. Structurally, the

shell of the house had suffered from years of leaks, dry rot, a lack of insulation, drafty single-glazed windows, and outdated heating, plumbing and electrical systems. Basically, the entire structure needed a serious upgrade, especially to meet today's hurricane and energy codes.

An obvious question: why did the new owners not just throw up their hands and tear the existing house down? These clients embraced the historic aesthetic and the unique opportunity to transform the house into a more livable, gracious and updated home. They loved the area for its historic houses and its preserved neighborhoods, and this house in particular for its siting on the top of the bluff. Together we decided to dig in and down (literally) and re-envision a home for the twenty-first century that preserved its original nineteenth-century aesthetic and heritage.

One of our first tasks was to come up with a more appealing entrance sequence. The solution was to raise the level of the ground at the old rear side of the house by five feet to establish a proper entry court. Lush landscaping and plantings at the entrance, and a half flight of stairs to a new porch and front door, now create entry at the main level while still providing light to the spaces below.

Next, we looked more closely at the shell of the house. With Dominick Pilla, an engineer with whom I often work, we designed an entirely new basic structure to provide a sound home. While we completely redesigned the interior with several major interventions, those are stories for another time. Here, I will focus mostly on the major structural improvements and exterior renovations.

Once we had established the new design, the first step was for Rich Kissane, our contractor, to carefully insert, in stages, the engineered-wood-and-steel structure into the shell, and tie it to the new concrete foundation. This would reinforce the house to meet all applicable local building and hurricane codes. No small undertaking, it meant temporarily supporting the entire structure on timber cribbing (see photos), allowing them to dig beneath it to form the new footings and concrete foundation. At the same time we were able to lower the original partial basement and crawl spaces and transform these into living spaces. Decidedly less cave-like, this newly expanded lower level, replete with higher ceilings, windows and French doors that open up under the protection of the porches above, accommodates a playroom, game room, bedroom, home theater, laundry and new mechanical rooms.

Above left: The west, water-facing side, which was the original 1880s entrance.

Top: The same view with the porch removed. The cribbing allowed the house to remain in place while the new foundation and basement were excavated.

Middle: Excavation beneath the first floor to create the new full-height living spaces in the basement.

Bottom: A new foundation was built while the structure was supported on timber cribs.

After

Before

After

Before

Opposite: The east facade,
before and after.

This page: The west facade,
before and after.

On the first-floor exterior, we rebuilt the porch, raising its roofline and extending it around three elevations. We replaced the leaky single-pane windows with insulated hurricane-resistant versions; adding new box bay windows — all preserving the authentic look.

We then focused on better connecting the indoors with the outdoors. On the main level, to access the new wrap-around porch, French doors with pocketing screens were added and the porch columns were relocated to ensure that they did not block views. The eave line was raised so that light now streams into the house. One of the key features of this new porch is the addition of a three-quarter round extension off the northwest corner that serves as a new outdoor living space, offering a beautiful panorama and continuous breezes.

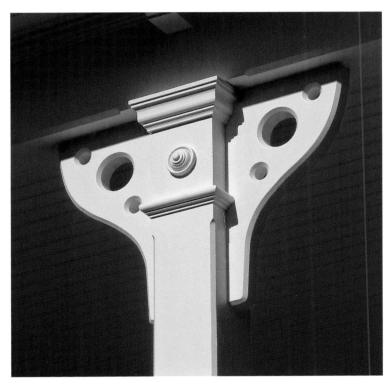

Opposite: Where the original east facade had presented as three-and-a-half stories tall, our design raised the ground level five feet and added an entry court, reducing the perception of the elevation to two-and-a-half stories. The basement is concealed under large porches on brick piers, yet natural light can filter in.

The exterior of the remaining two upper stories required a renewal of all finishes — clapboard was replaced, modern insulation and waterproofing added, original ornament was documented and recreated. New millwork features were added after thorough research: an oriel window over the front door and a window seat in the stair hall; a box bay that expands the living room, complete with ornamental transom windows; and a similar bay to extend the new main floor kitchen to include a breakfast annex. This work involved replacing all of the windows with new hurricane-resistant divided-light versions designed to be stylistically consistent with the age of the house, but to meet the wind loads and projectile tests. We also reintroduced functioning shutters that actually close and lock to protect against storms, and finally and literally capping this off, a new roof was installed.

Opposite: The new porch serves as a light-filled outdoor living space with stunning views.

This page: A greatly expanded porch offers abundant space for entertaining and enjoying the wide vistas and fresh breezes.

Bottom: The existing Poolhouse and pool beyond, barely visible.

Opposite and this page, top: The renovated pool and new Poolhouse, adjacent to the new entry court but a half-level lower. Inviting gardens and landscape design enhance the separation of these areas.

Not all of the exterior redesign was driven to meet codes and wind loads — we also had some fun. In the spirit of the "new" oriel windows, we recreated the feel of the century-old feature of a sleeping porch by carving a sitting area out of the west, water-side portion of the second-floor elevation. Privately accessed, it is a well-used extension of the master bedroom.

I recommended the landscape architect Peter Cummin and his team to redesign the grounds, a reorganization that was almost as extensive as the renovation of the house. Retaining walls were built to level off parts of the property that had been deeply sloping; making them usable for entertaining and play. We also planted mature trees and hedges to better frame sight lines. What had originally been a rather restricted exterior experience is now far more inviting and private. Peter planted mature trees, privet hedges and evergreen shrubs to better define these spaces and frame sight lines. While you can still see the house from a distance, when people approach along the road it disappears from view, significantly enhancing the family's privacy.

Remembering what this tired old house was like when I was first introduced to it, I am extremely pleased with how we transformed it. My clients showed real vision and determination in choosing to invest so much time, energy and resources to this rejuvenation, and were rewarded with what has turned out to be an ideal summer home.

Left: The house, early in the renovation process, raised on temporary cribbing before the entry court area was constructed on engineered fill and stone retaining walls.

Crafting Heritage

Architects are the creative force of buildings; we see ourselves as the people who "make" the project happen. But the reality is that the by-product of any architect's work is, well … a set of drawings. They have a lot of information on them, but they are just drawings on paper — that is our "deliverable." It falls to literally hundreds of other skilled people working with us to turn those drawings into a tangible structure.

Once our initial concepts and preliminary designs are approved by the client we begin to develop the design by collaborating with a supporting cast of highly accomplished professionals — landscape architects, interior designers and decorators, engineers, consultants and contractors — whose experiences and know-how help bring the design to a completed set of working drawings. But this ending point is really the starting point.

When construction starts, the first group on whom I rely are the dedicated subcontractors, excavators, concrete installers, steel workers, carpenters, electricians, tin knockers and plumbers who create the scene for the bespoke detail work for which my firm is known to follow: the virtuosi cabinetmakers, wood carvers, restorers, plasterers, stonecutters, marble cutters, masons, painters, wood finishers, among so many others. Speak to most any of them and you will discover that what they do is much more than a job, it is a passion. Thinking about it, their work is not signed; they are virtually anonymous. The homeowner probably does not know who framed the room much less who hand-carved the intricate moldings, and certainly no one who casually visits knows. Many work in relative obscurity for the joy of forming an intricate, delicate plaster medallion, or of carving a mahogany twisting newel post on a staircase, or an exceptional piece of millwork.

Over these many years, I have been fortunate to collaborate with extraordinary craftspeople, and what I learned from them about fine building is inestimable. This began in David Easton's studio in 1984, where I met Joe Marino. Joe was already in his eighties and had been working on fine homes for almost sixty years as an accomplished draftsman; he drew beautifully. Not only were his drawings thoughtfully composed but they also communicated solutions of the design detail to the builders in a way that gave them the information they needed, while leaving room for the

artist or craftsperson to apply their own talents and input as it was realized. Though I only worked alongside Joe for a short while, he was a priceless inspiration for a young architect.

It was at about this time I met the master plasterer Gabe Patrella. An older gentleman who had been at this craft for all of his life, he would take my architectural drawing, critique it, then model it in clay, refine it again and again, finally creating molds for casting; then a few weeks later, he had the finished plaster element set out on his bench, an object far more beautiful than the drawing had rendered it. You can see the use of both cast and run plaster in some of the projects featured in this book as I have had the chance to work with a number of quality ornamental plasterers: Hyde Park, Foster Reeve or Fresco in New York City, Balmer in Toronto, JP Philips in Chicago, and Troika in London among others. In collaboration with these artists, we have realized the designs for many ornamental cornices, overdoors and ceiling motifs.

Fine woodworking also calls for skills and techniques quickly being lost in this country. Woodworkers start with the architect's detail, transferring it to a shop drawing. There is often a back-and-forth to see how various elements can be milled, carved and assembled. With an approved shop drawing, whenever possible, we will look to get mock-ups made for our review and client approval. This is when (apparently) I've been known to tweak or enhance the details. We are now ready for the rough timber to be procured, planed, trimmed, molded, shaped, carved, assembled and sometimes hand finished: what began as a pile of lumber on a loading dock becomes an amazing pine library, or raised-panel crotch veneer mahogany doors, or kitchen cabinets, fully fit out to meet the expectations of both the amateur cook or professional chef.

A few of these millworkers really stand out. About twenty-five years ago David and I were asked to create a very high-style classical French apartment on the Upper East Side of Manhattan. During this time we were introduced to Jean Pierre Fancelli, a French woodworker, skilled in the design, carving and fabrication of authentic boiserie. Jean Pierre, whose workshop was in Paris, had created work for private clients and as well historic restoration, he had even done some of the restoration at the Palace of Versailles, where I had studied as an undergraduate. Over the course of the apartment project I had the great fortune to visit Jean Pierre's shop in Paris several times.

One afternoon we took a "field trip" to Versailles where he showed me some of the rooms he had restored, as well as some that were still in progress. It was amazing to see this historic boiserie— most in decent condition and all of it presenting the design vocabulary that we were now trying to replicate over three-hundred-and-fifty years later.

Charles Manners is another uniquely skilled woodworker with whom I have collaborated on several projects in the U.S., Canada and the U.K. Charles has crafted amazing works for us, such as the Nordic pine library in California (shown earlier), which is of wood obtained from trees grown above the Arctic Circle; a gothic-inspired European oak study/office with carved cornices and moldings; full houses of hand-scraped and polished English brown oak plank floors; and, changing style entirely, the highly specialized Ruhlmann-inspired macassar ebony and mahogany dressing room for the Lakefront Apartment (also featured in this book). All were within the artistic reach of Charles' shop. Virtually all of these pieces were hand-worked in his studio in Shropshire, England, where using full-sized templates from the site they would construct the entire room. He would then have it transported to the site where it was painstakingly installed by Charles and his team. Another great asset in our collaboration is that someone like Charles is more than a gifted cabinetmaker and restorer. His is part of a very exclusive network of carvers, restorers, polishers and timber suppliers, enabling him to source the finest raw materials and talent for projects.

Stone and marble carvers are still another group of true, old-world artists who contribute to our fine entry halls, master bathrooms, kitchens, custom mantels, and bars. Almost anyone in the field can do flat work and milled-edge profiles, which are now cut on sophisticated, computerized, multi-axis machinery. But when it comes to hand-carved custom work, particularly on a mantel, the list is very short. A client of ours in Connecticut, a businessman with a lifelong interest in poetry who was about to retire, planned to devote his retirement to this passion. When he and his wife purchased their new home in Greenwich, a house that we had renovated years before for the previous owner, he contacted me, asking us to re-work the living room mantel, making it much more personal. I designed a hooded over-mantel supported by a pair of corbeled legs onto which he requested the faces of Dante and Aristotle. Here I called Dan Sinclair, an extremely talented carver

who took this project very much to heart. Dan did extensive research, then modeled the faces in clay for review before carving in French limestone. I visited this client not long ago. Twenty years later he was as enamored of these carvings as he had been when they were first installed.

I should note that craftsmanship isn't always about fine ornamental finishes. When we designed the Low Country Plantation, the final project in this book, it was critical that both the Game House and Horse Barn be constructed with true exposed, historically-inspired timber frames to get the expression I was looking for. We had worked with of a group of very skilled timber wrights from Vermont Timberworks who we knew would be able to produce the hand-hewn structural timbers, ceiling joists and trusses. But soon happily learned that they were able to completely conceal the required steel-bolted hurricane connections, thus ensuring the aged look and feel of a true timber frame.

These are only a few examples of the many, many superb craftspeople that we have had the chance to work with over the past 30 years. There are so many others: the metal workers, like John O'Brien, Pivot Etc., Focal Metals, who cast our balustrades or line our countertops with zinc; the tile setters lining a shower with moroccan mosaics; the custom hardware suppliers, such as E.R. Butler, Nanz, and Katonah; the crafting of a herringbone or parquet de Versailles reclaimed oak floor by Stephen Gamble, William Erbe or Heritage Floors; or of course the terrific painters and faux finishers who makes it all look perfect at the end.

As you page through the homes in this book, take a moment to reflect on that what you are seeing may have begun with the sketch or drawing of the architect, but could never have become the photo that you see without the skill, care and passion of the craftsman. I regard my chances to collaborate with these committed individuals as one of the most satisfying aspect of my practice — and I believe every one of our clients would agree they have benefited from the results.

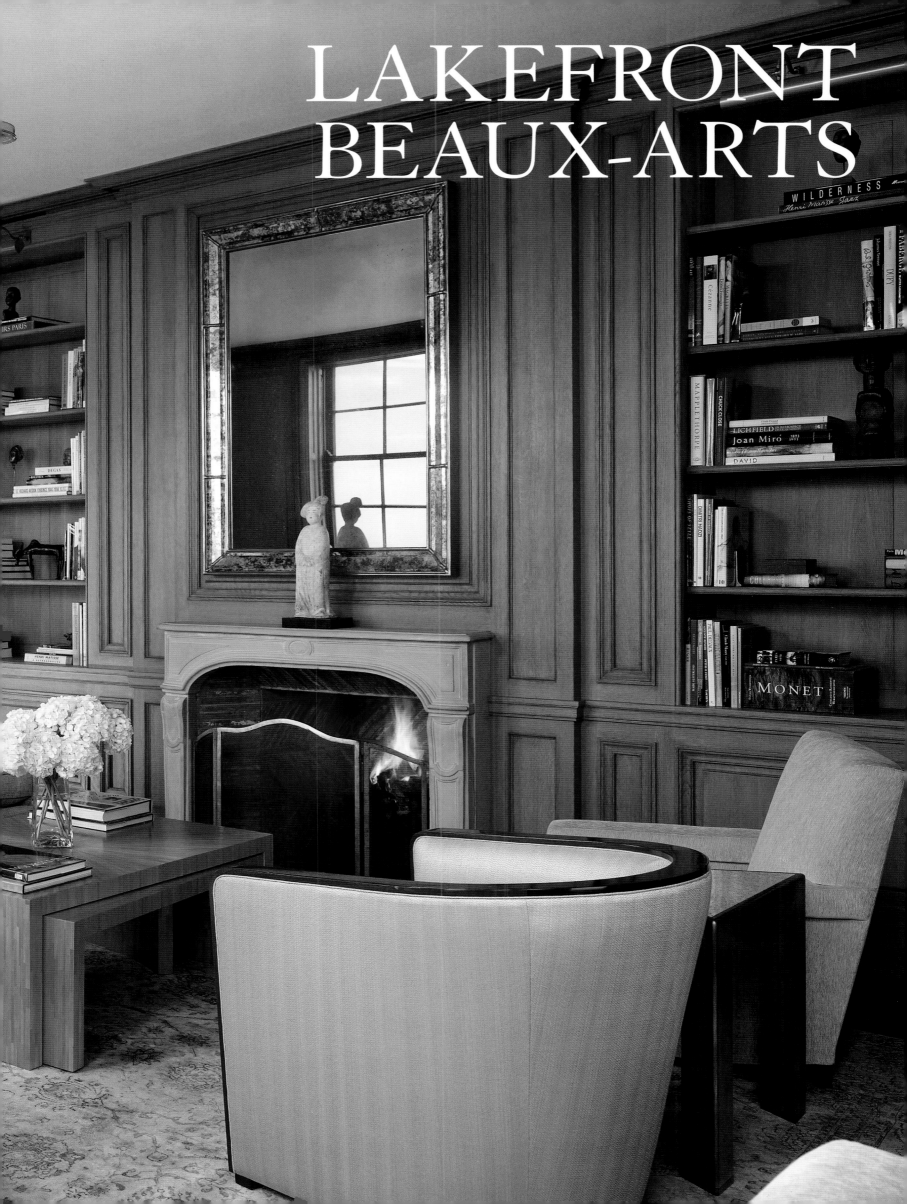

LAKEFRONT
BEAUX-ARTS

Above: This magnificent 1911 apartment building was carved up in the 1960s, destroying the original single-floor apartments with their classic French details, creating instead four nondescript units per floor. In this case, my clients were patient and persevering, and were able to assemble three of the four units on one floor that we recombined into a single apartment.

Beaux-Arts-inspired boiserie panels in all of the main rooms — entry hall, living room, library, master suite, and kitchen — was a consistent element on which the owners could display their art collection. We chose French limestone for the floor of the entry, serving as the transition from outside to interior, and to balance the strong geometries of the paneling and oak parquet de Versailles floors beyond.

ENTRY HALL

I was commissioned to create this home in a lakefront Chicago apartment house for a soon-to-be-retired couple, who were looking to make a major lifestyle change — leaving the family home and vertical lifestyle of a nearby townhouse for the easier horizontal living of an apartment.

The twelve-story building, designed in 1911 by Benjamin Marshall, is a beautiful Beaux-Arts–inspired terra-cotta structure. Part of what makes it so desirable is that it stands alone within the block, with marvelous exposures on every side. Marshall was also responsible for some of the city's most beautiful and distinctive prewar architecture, including its famous Drake and Blackstone hotels. When this building opened, each floor featured a single apartment of about 7,500 square feet, creating a full home on one level and designed with an ornate sensibility. Sometime in the 1960s, it was converted to condominiums and these commodious apartments were divided into four nondescript units per floor. Almost all of the original interior detailing was lost.

Living differently than the original occupants did in 1911, the couple didn't employ a staff of five, or dress for formal dinners each evening, but as they entertain quite often for charity, they wanted public rooms that flowed easily one into another. In addition to a couple of graciously-sized guest suites, they desired private spaces for themselves. David Easton and I were recommended by their builder, with whom they had recently worked on their weekend house. The builder had worked with us on another Chicago apartment renovation a few years earlier. He'd been impressed by not only how smoothly the renovation had gone, but also by the level of detail and design resolution we achieved. The prospect of starting a redesign in this historic building was a great thrill, having worked in Chicago early in my career on a David Adler–designed house that featured true Beaux-Arts design, and having studied in Versailles as a student.

These clients were very fortunate, very strategic, and very patient, and over a number of years were able to assemble three of the four units on the same floor. Veterans of several major construction projects, they wanted a design team who could sensitively reestablish the beauty of the apartment as if it had been original, but in a manner that would support their twenty-first century lives.

We inherited three working fireplaces and four balconies but also old plumbing, electrical and air-conditioning systems; as there was little worth saving, the units were gutted. The clients enjoyed the building's French facade and hoped for an interior with a similar but more restrained French sophistication. The cue would come from the building's lobby, a wonderfully distinctive, two-story orangerie-like space with a big beautiful fireplace. It was this space that we would use as inspiration for the design of the new apartment, creating an aesthetic connection from building entry to their new home.

We created an interior with a formality suggested by the original floor plan, reestablishing the view to the exterior upon entering the apartment. Instead of designing a "grand salon" and "petite salon," we integrated a living room and library. Among the glories of this building, none are more unique than the two generously sized semi-circular bays on each floor. We turned the one in the living room into an intimate dining space with extraordinary views of the lake; the couple did not want a separate formal dining room. The other bay became the master sitting room.

With respect to the exterior, one of the first things we had to deal with were the original windows, which leaked when intense storms blew in from Lake Michigan. As the building is in a historic district, the new windows had to resemble the old, but luckily they didn't have to function the same way. Previously, if you wanted to go out on the balconies, you had to awkwardly open triple-hung windows, and people tended to hit their heads on the bottom of the second rail. We designed divided-light French doors that looked just like the original windows but functioned as true doors, making the balconies far more accessible and enjoyable.

Left: The library, featuring French oak paneling and integrated bookcases, serves as both an intimate sitting area and a media room with concealed TV and surround sound. All open onto a north-facing balcony and views of the water.

Above: The library connects to the living room with symmetrical Harmon-hinged doors, and we thickened walls to reinforce the sense of an old-world masonry building.

Left: The two generous semi-circular bays on each floor are original to the building. We adapted the bay at the end of the living room to become the dining "room." The client chose to forgo a formal dining room, preferring the more relaxed lifestyle and multifunctional space to a separate formal dining room. The large table is also an outstanding space for puzzle building.

Above: The solidity of the oak paneling is revealed as an illusion when it becomes the hidden door to a china closet.

One of the distinctive aspects of this apartment is the use of paneling in nearly every room. The boiserie was ideally suited to hanging artwork, an important concern for these clients. As we do with most projects, we made half-inch scale models of all the rooms. We placed the art, to scale, in each model room to ensure that the proportions of the panel and artwork suited each other.

The public spaces are separated from the private by a gallery that creates ample space for much of their art collection. To add warmth to the public areas, the boiserie was crafted with oak from northern Germany, one of the few places where you can still get timber from generations-old trees possessing a very tight grain. That's ideal as it gives the paneling a much more refined coloration, absorbs the finish exceedingly well and has an immediate sense of age. The oak was sourced by the millworker, Bob Parenti, who visited the mill during a European holiday, and whose shop produced most of the paneling and cabinetry. In the private rooms we chose a painted panel vocabulary and worked closely with Erik R. Smith in David Easton's office who developed a tone-on-tone glaze.

To complement the strong geometries of the paneling, we suggested French limestone for the floor in the entry, and a mix of parquet de Versailles and oak planks, both hand-scraped and finished to give the floors in the balance of the main rooms the lustre of decades-old patina. The ceiling plane was kept very simple with just a bit of ornament, and run plaster cornices in the painted spaces.

Above: The couple wanted a family kitchen furnished with a center table and comfortable seating. With access to one of the balconies, the room is the center of the apartment.

Opposite: The transition from private to public space is achieved through the use of the gallery that terminates the entry hall art sequence with a pair of doors. These introduce the private quarters, which include the master suite and two guest bedrooms.

Interestingly, it was the husband who requested be included some real deco glamour in the apartment, while his wife asked for a lighter, softer, more Belle Epoque feeling. Accordingly, we designed different dressing and bathroom suites for each. In her suite we used clean lines of painted panels and moldings to maintain continuity with the master bedroom, and David used a tone-on-tone glaze to enhance their shape and shadow. For his dressing room, we researched the furnishings and interiors of the elegant French Art Deco designer Émile-Jacques Ruhlmann. Rather than buy a breakfront or some other work of his for the husband's rooms, we decided to design an entire suite in the spirit of Ruhlmann. The husband was very keen on its design; being involved pleased him immensely. Ruhlmann, of course, used ivory and other rare materials for inlay, but that is now out of the question; instead, we collaborated with British woodworker Charles Manners, who built and installed these rooms, to source shaved camel bone, which we paired with macassar ebony and mahogany, favorite materials of Ruhlmann.

Many of my clients enjoy being part of the design and building process, and these clients were particularly interested and involved, especially the husband, who had retired from business just as we began, remaining active in philanthropy with a special interest in public education. After the project was completed, he paid me one of the highest compliments I've ever received. He told me that he really enjoyed the experience of "guided discovery" that I had brought to the project, adding "You know Eric, that's how all the best teachers teach." I had never thought of it that way, but it was deeply gratifying to have him connect that idea with my work.

Opposite: In a traditional free-standing home, the second floor becomes the obvious transition from public space to private. In an apartment, one has to achieve this through the use of hallways and galleries to create connection as well as separation.

Here, the gallery extends the space of the entry and, at the same time, terminates it in a private hallway that leads to the master suite, guest suite, and exercise room.

Above: The master suite, in addition to the bedroom, separate bath and dressing rooms, also makes use of the second large bay window as a sitting room and office space for the husband.

Opposite: The private quarters, which include the master suite and two guest bedrooms, are reached through a pair of doors that mark the end of the gallery, terminating the entry hall art sequence.

Above: Her bathroom extends the detailing of the master bedroom with clean lines and a tone-on-tone palette.

MR. DRESSING

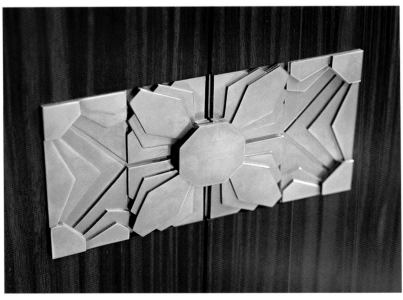

Opposite and this page: My sketch for the husband's dressing room, which was inspired by the work of Émile-Jacques Ruhlmann, the noted Parisian Art Deco designer. The geometries and lines, decorative insets and proportions of this cabinetry are all inspired by his work. We worked very closely with master cabinetmaker Charles Manners on the meticulous detailing and sourcing the perfect materials.

Right: Our clients are very active in several charitable organizations and often entertain. This light-filled living area is generous and spacious, but allows for intimate conversation. We worked closely with David Easton's office, especially with Erik R. Smith, who hewed to a muted, neutral but elegant palette for the rugs, upholstery and textiles.

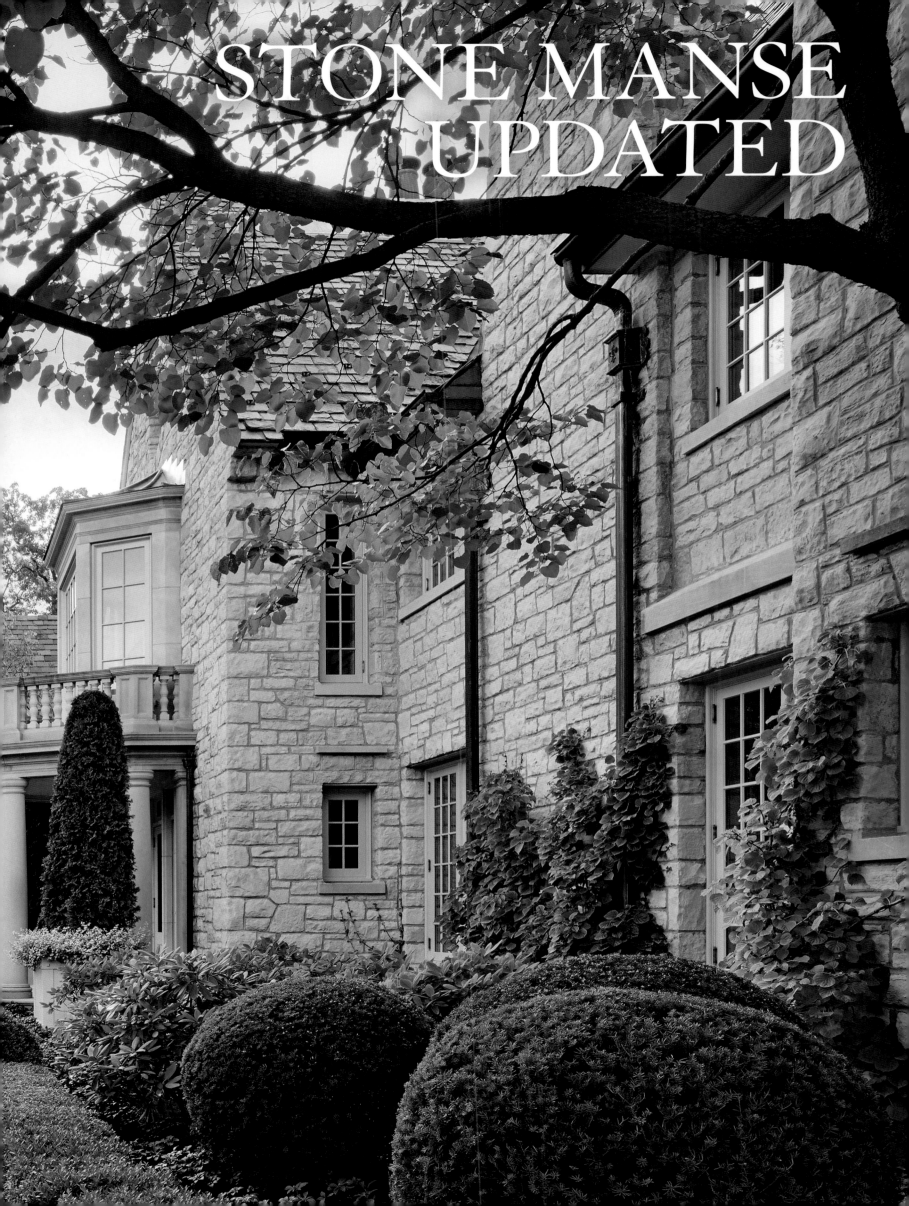

STONE MANSE UPDATED

Many years ago and in collaboration with David Easton, we designed a vacation home on a stunning property in Colorado with spectacular views of the Elk Mountains for a family from Chicago. It was a large, complicated, and ultimately very successful project. The trust that developed between the owners and the design team during the building of that house led them to ask us to design the renovation of their primary residence, a Cotswold-inspired 1920s stone house on the North Shore. With their children now getting ready to embark on lives of their own, the couple thought it was time to address the many longstanding issues they had with the family home.

When originally built, the house had been constructed of reinforced concrete and steel with a limestone veneer and slate roof. At that time, people chose this form of construction as it made a house more fire-resistant than conventional wood; this was at a time when fire departments were often miles away. In this case, the result was a veritable bunker with little detail and even less natural light. The existing concrete structure would prove to make any kind of renovation quite a challenge.

Faced with a renovation as lengthy and complicated as this one promised to be, many homeowners might have simply moved, but this couple felt deeply attached to their home and neighborhood. The wife had been pregnant with her youngest son when they first moved in; it was where they had raised their children. They knew too that they could never find another house in the area as commodious. Even though they would soon be empty nesters, they hoped that someday their extra bedrooms would be used by their grown children, grandchildren, and extended families.

The clients had done some renovation work years earlier when they first moved in, but the systems had never been properly upgraded, nor had the dark interiors and awkward flow been resolved. Our renovation would be far more than simply updating bathrooms and kitchens or installing new mechanicals; it was a complete overhaul and re-envisioning of the home, which ultimately included the grounds and main approach from the road.

To determine how best to improve the flow and continuity of the spaces while also bringing more daylight in, we spent a great deal of time studying the existing plan, fenestration and finishes. Once our new plan was approved, we had the interiors stripped down to the concrete and steel structure. The original construction put such severe constraints on potential renovation schemes that I relied mostly on surgical-style interventions to brighten and enhance the rooms: this included punching out new or larger windows, adding a series of skylights with lay lights, and changing the floor heights in several areas.

At the front entry, we added a semi-hexagonal stone porch that welcomes and protects visitors from bad weather. Changing the solid-wood front door to one that is partially glazed and adding sidelights with mirrored panels, the entry took on a whole new life. Above the porch we extended the stair landing with a bay window and inserted an oculus to provide more daylight inside and detail outside, enlivening what had previously been a flat-front facade.

Some of our first design gestures were to enliven the front elevation. We added an oculus, a bay window at the landing of the front stairway, and a new front porch, replacing the solid wood door with a partial-glass front door and sidelights. These moves transformed the entry experience by adding dimension to the facade and bringing needed light into the house.

RENEWING TRADITION

Above: The main staircase and entry are now flooded with light from the new front vestibule, a second-floor bay window and skylight. Pocketing wood doors provide evening privacy.

Left: The main stair was updated by adding a new bronze balustrade. The portal that leads into the living room and the library beyond establishes the cross-axis to the front hall.

One of our most significant interior changes was the lowering of the living room floor. Doing this, and simultaneously exposing and celebrating the existing ceiling beams by adding smaller secondary beams, created a better-proportioned and more richly textured room. As part of the redesign, we enlarged the front-facing windows, added window seats, and designed a bay window opposite the fireplace, extending the house toward the garden. Taking advantage of the two massive columns we inherited from the original structure, we added two L-shaped banquettes to create an internal division of seating areas. Large areas of wall space lit by fiber optics provide flexible display options for an ever-changing art collection. Today the room's airy feel and myriad views of trees and greenery make it one of the couple's most used spaces.

Left, top, and next pages: We worked carefully with the original concrete-and-steel structure to raise the ceiling heights and inserted more and larger windows on both sides of the living room, including a box bay with full-height glass, directly opposite the fireplace. English oak herringbone floors provide a subtle undertexture to the carpets and furniture.

The main axis from the entry continues through to the large picture window over the library fireplace.

Above: My original sketch for the living room, before we decided to expose the existing beams and add decorative crossbeams for scale.

MR STUDY

Left: The coup of the library's design is the new fireplace with the picture window directly above. The view is on axis with the doorways from the living room and entry, and is enhanced by mirrored window jambs. The library also contains a home office. The design allows all work materials to be neatly stored out of view behind metal-grilled-and-framed doors. We were fortunate to work with Charles Manners. He fabricated and installed all of the carved crown molding and European oak millwork.

Above: My initial sketch, before committing to a fully oak-paneled room with carved quatrefoil cornice.

Opposite and above: Part of the owners' art collection is displayed in a first-floor main gallery, which connects the entry hall with the private areas of the house, and in an intersecting secondary gallery. Fiber optic lighting is employed in both spaces because it can be easily adjusted.

Left: We transformed the kitchen, reducing its footprint and creating separate space for food and butler's pantries. This resulted in a smaller, better proportioned, and more functional kitchen. It is now suffused with daylight from a large central skylight, picture window, and glass-fronted cabinets with frosted glass backs.

Skylights are an excellent device for bringing daylight into the interior of a space. We added these in the kitchen and, paired with frosted glass laylights, they suffuse the kitchen with natural light. This required some architectural gymnastics as well as some clever structural adjustments to the roof. To heighten the effect of natural light in the kitchen without compromising storage, we used a design feature we had employed in their vacation house; glass-fronted cabinets with frosted glass backs and sides, which we set into windows so that natural light streams through them. It's a very unusual technique, but quite effective in brightening the room.

The work we did in the basement gave us the opportunity to design a large wine cellar and a state-of-the-art media room, which has become a favorite haunt of the husband. To accomplish this, we moved the exercise room from the basement to the second floor, which works well for the couple, who are exercise enthusiasts. For convenience we added a small second-floor laundry room. The wife has joked that, with the purchase of a small fridge, she could live entirely on that floor.

Above: The kitchen is the family center of the house but must be able to function for a professional chef for events. The new kitchen is smaller, more functional and light-filled than the original.

Opposite: The butler's pantry, with a historically inspired mahogany counter, serves as a buffer to the dining room and also as a bar area.

Top: We created a large game space and informal eating area by extending the family room toward the garden. Lit by a combination of French doors and windows and a new skylight, the space is effectively wrapped by daylight on four sides.

Right: The more private family spaces begin with the family room that connects the entry gallery, the art gallery and the garden room.

The interior designer Erik R. Smith played an important role in re-envisioning the décor of this home which together we lightened, brightened and enlivened. This was not the first time Erik R., as we call him, and I had collaborated; he was part of the David Easton team that had worked on the couple's Colorado home and had started this project with David's office. Happily, we are usually of one mind in our design approach and while the mountain house had been decorated in more traditional Tuscan and Provençal styles, in the intervening years the couple had begun collecting modern and contemporary art, so a cleaner, simpler decor was appropriate to showcase their paintings and sculptures. Erik R. augmented their collection of antique furnishings with some eclectic French pieces, such as a fine parchment side table by Jacques Adnet in the entry, and an antique Persian rug in pale tones in the living room. Stripping out the dark finishes throughout the house and replacing them with lighter woods, the ivory tones for the walls and English brown-oak floors served to brighten the entire interior.

We also completely overhauled a little-used and awkwardly proportioned two-story space on the perimeter of the house into a sunlit orangerie-inspired garden room, now a beloved retreat. To accomplish this transformation, we coved the flat ceiling, bringing the space down and switched out the nondescript fenestration for Palladian-style steel windows that reference the 1920s. This space, like much of the house, is kept cozy during Chicago winters by new radiant heating. The pleasing proportions, generous fenestration, and careful placement of two architectural axes all work together to draw the garden deep into the house. The room feels intimate even when sitting in it alone.

Above: We designed a bar on the interior wall of the garden room with a mirror that reflects the garden.

RENEWING TRADITION

A few years after we finished renovating this client's primary home on Chicago's North Shore, they mentioned that they were considering the purchase of an apartment in New York City to use as a pied-à-terre. They had grown tired of staying in hotels and had been using the one-bedroom apartment in Greenwich Village that one of their sons had vacated when he left New York. Traveling to New York more frequently for both business and pleasure, the couple decided it was time to acquire a larger apartment. A three-bedroom apartment was available in a nearby building that was being converted to condominiums. Once the apartment was under contract they looked to the same design team — me as architect and Erik R. Smith as interior designer — to create their new pied-à-terre.

In the years since we had designed their Chicago house, the couple had adopted a more contemporary taste in art and design. Now a trustee on a couple of art museum boards, the wife spent a good deal of time with other collectors, many of whom had extremely modern homes. Intrigued by the "less is more" aesthetic she was seeing, she wanted to experiment with living in a spare, minimalist environment that would serve as both a serene retreat and a dramatic showplace for art and entertaining.

We conceived the apartment as a restrained study in surfaces and textures, an environment that would intrigue with its subtlety while serving as a flexible backdrop to the couple's rotating, ever-growing art collection.

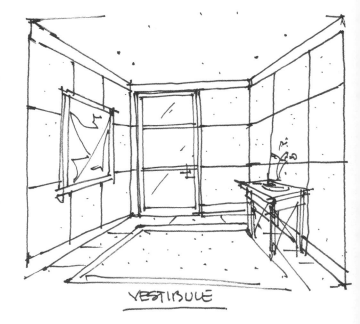

VESTIBULE

Opposite: The elevator lets out directly into this private vestibule. This simple composition points to the Jeff Koons *Monkey* that is the focal point of the end of the gallery beyond. The study of light and texture are introduced by the luminous quality of the front door and the stone plank floor. An extraordinary amount of care was required to prepare walls of parchment panels and to cantilever a flush, glass-slab shelf at the entry wall.

Above: My original design sketch for the entry vestibule. The free-standing table has been replaced by the glass-slab shelf, and the more traditional flooring patterns by full-width limestone planks that visually reinforce the path of travel.

Right: Mid-century modern furniture and a dramatic, vintage Austrian chandelier in the dining room were sourced by Erik R. Smith, who designed additional complementary pieces.

The trimless architecture, including white stone sills, subtly conceals heating and cooling systems, electrical outlets and pocket doors. Mirrored window jambs reflect the cityscape and magnify natural light. The walls in each room feature various textures of hand-finished plaster, scour brushed and polished.

RENEWING TRADITION

Left and above: The original 1905 building's proportions are apparent in the living room, which showcases stunning modern art by Ellsworth Kelly and Louise Lawler. Above the fireplace, a lacquered panel retracts to reveal a large-screen TV (above) that can extend and rotate on a mechanical arm for full-room viewing.

Top: Glazed pocket doors slide open to reveal all of the spaces, in this case a small private office.

Previous pages and top: The enfilade from the kitchen through the dining and living rooms parallels that of the gallery. Every intersection and every change of material was meticulously considered.

Right: Etched-glass pocket doors slide closed for private dining. All of the doors in the public rooms are highly engineered, with double-pane etched glass, that are both beautiful and add to the acoustic separation between the rooms.

Opposite: The U-shaped plan of the apartment organizes public space along one side, with the gallery serving as transition between public and private.

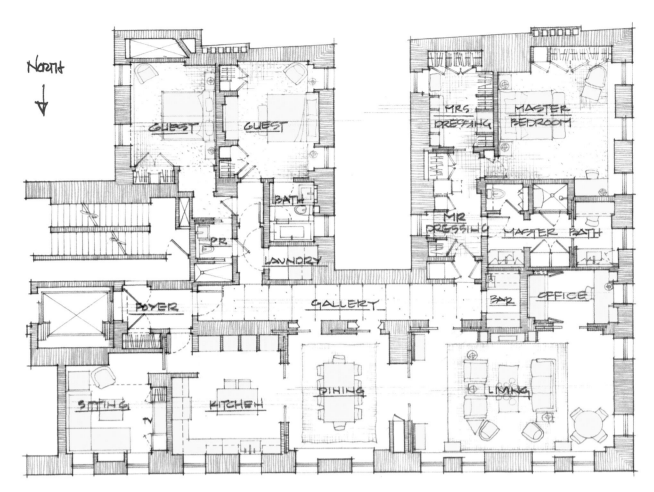

The building, erected in 1905, had been built as a safe and respectable residence for young working women; in the 1950s it became a facility for the elderly. Now it was being repurposed into luxury apartments that, while generous in size, were not ideally configured; they had low ceilings with ill-placed soffits. Transforming the existing set of rooms into an interior that was light and airy was a challenge. Our solution was to open up the space and to organize the apartment as series of sliding "boxes," where rooms disappear and reappear via a series of etched-glass pocket doors. They are engineered with minimal, beautifully-detailed frames to produce thin sight lines. Though weighing hundreds of pounds each, they can be moved with a single finger.

Our goal of creating a sleek, light-filled central gallery, defining an enfilade of public rooms on one side and two separate bedroom wings on the other side, was aided immeasurably by a concurrent renovation in the apartment immediately above. The upstairs neighbors were hoping to move plumbing that was also creating some unfortunate drops in our ceilings. In accommodating the changes they desired, we were able to create one smooth contiguous ceiling plane — reinforcing the clean volumes of the public spaces, and eliminating the intrusions in our ceilings.

By utilizing fiber-optic lighting throughout much of the apartment, we were able to preserve ceiling heights and provide flexibility and adjustability to accommodate the art collection as it changes.

The etched-glass sliding doors let light move through the space even when they are closed; the clients appreciate their elegant versatility. When they are home alone or have a house guest, the clients can close off the kitchen, dining room and/or living rooms to create smaller, more private spaces; when they are entertaining large groups for cocktails or dinner, they can open the doors to transform the apartment into an open-plan, gallery-like scheme.

Left and above: In the kitchen, oak cabinet surfaces were horizontally wire-brushed, then stained gray and further cerused to achieve a soft, textured finish. Matching panels conceal the refrigerator and pantry on the right, while a textured metallic tile backsplash accentuates the cooking area.

Top: The hidden secondary "door" in the entry vestibule provides family access to the kitchen and small sitting room.

Left and above: Design themes established in the public spaces recur in the master bedroom, where simple planar geometries, concealed storage, natural light, stunning modern art, and mid-century modern fixtures coalesce in a peaceful, gracious urban sanctuary. Mirrored window jambs combine with bedside mirrors to amplify natural light and enhance a sense of reflection and dimensional space.

Following pages: The master dressing room and bath complete the suite. As in the main living spaces, sliding doors are used in here with a combination of lacquered and natural wood panels.

Working in a minimalist style was challenging and exhilarating. For me, it was like walking a high wire because the requirements were so exacting. In our more traditional work, a variety of trims can be used to cover joints and edges, and ease transitions. Here, every aspect of the design was exposed and had to be absolutely perfect. Fortunately, we worked with Eammon Ryan of Nordic Builders, who understood this and executed our designs to perfection.

Above: The east guest bath, accessed by both the gallery and guest bedroom, functions most often as an elegant powder room; its full shower hidden by a sliding lacquered wall-panel converts it to a full bath.

Right: There are two guest bedrooms; both boast iconic Roy Lichtenstein prints. Textiles and paint colors were selected by Erik R. Smith to relate to the art. Jib closet doors allow the wall surfaces to be continuous on all sides of the room.

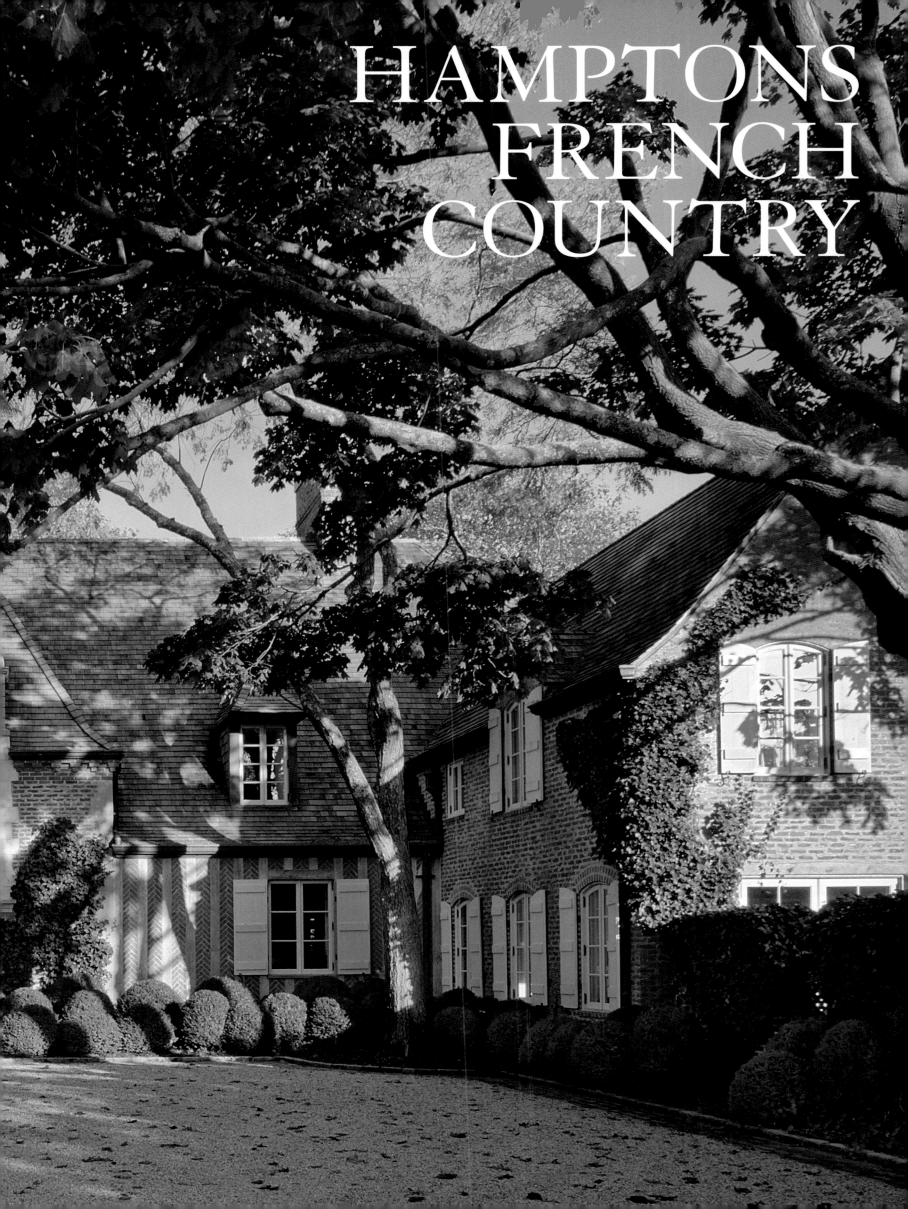

HAMPTONS
FRENCH
COUNTRY

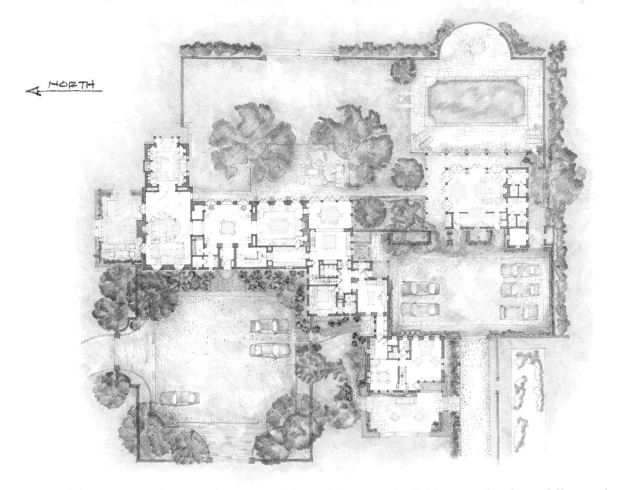

NORTH

One of the greatest pleasures in my work is reviving wonderful houses that have fallen on hard times. That was the case with this marvelous Normandy-style home in the Hamptons that had been neglected for many years. Like so many great old houses, it had a rich backstory. The New York society firm Polhemus & Coffin, which specialized in château-style buildings in the early twentieth century, designed it along with a companion house in the same French country style on a contiguous property with a shared driveway. This handsome property featured the Main House; a fanciful brick Gatehouse at the entry with Normandy details; a Guesthouse, built in the midcentury and adjacent to the main residence; and a Poolhouse that had been added later. The property bounds one of the Hamptons' many pretty coastal lakes; the ocean is so close you can hear the roar of the surf — but without sand getting blown in your eyes.

My clients were a husband and wife with a young daughter. They had originally wanted a Shingle-style weekend house and had to be cajoled by the broker to see this property. On seeing the house they were immediately smitten and became determined to restore it to its former glory, which definitely took some imagination. The property needed owners with passion, commitment, and patience because so much had to be repaired, replaced, and rethought. Before setting off on a serious renovation, I caution clients that even though a house may be standing and functioning, it will almost certainly be a lengthier and often as much or more expensive a project than a new construction. I also remind them of the rewards for their investment and patience, as they gain a house with a history — and often a mature setting and an intriguing pedigree — that has now been custom-tailored to suit their lives and families.

Our work on this house began with making the house watertight. First, a new roof and flashings had to be installed, with repairs made to the chimney. Next were repairs to the "nogging" — the term for brickwork set within a timber frame — one of this house's most distinctive features. Both brick and timber were in bad shape and had to be replaced in some places and repointed most everywhere else.

Opposite: One of the first steps of the renovation was the repair of the nogging, a traditional system of brickwork set within a timber frame that is one of this home's most distinctive features.

Working with the landscape architect Deborah Nevins, the entry court was revived. Belgian block curbs and gutters frame the gravel driving surface. Mounded boxwoods provide a transition from exterior to interior.

Above: Our initial design for the site presented architectural changes, integration of furniture and preliminary landscape concepts simultaneously to illustrate the connection between all three.

Above: In addition to the Main House, there are several outbuildings, some original, others not. The property is directly on one of the many "ponds" found along the ocean beaches in the Hamptons.

ENTRY VESTIBULE.

Opposite: The view from the front door through the entry to the east lawn and pond beyond. The reclaimed limestone pavers, set in a running bond pattern, lend texture and age to the entry hall.

Left: My initial sketch, showing the connection of spaces and introducing the French-inspired paneled interiors.

Above: The cross axis of the entry hall connects the living room and dining room. Many houses built in the 1920s tend to have dark rooms, small windows and low ceilings; much of our work focused on opening the home to natural light and creating a sense of space.

Above: The dining room continues the enfilade of water-facing spaces. We replaced smaller windows with pairs of transomed French doors to optimize light and view. Pocketing screens are hidden when not in use.

Opposite: The large arched portal opens from the living room across from and on-axis with a new matching portal to the dining room, forming a symmetrical axial relationship. The two steps down announce an increase of space achieved by lowering the floor by a foot.

We started on the interior by addressing some of the most pressing design issues. Like many houses built in the 1920s, the inside was quite dark. In addition to replacing the existing windows, we enlarged a number of them to become French doors, allowing in more daylight. We also punched out some of the rear walls to insert French doors that take better advantage of the water views.

As the mechanical systems of the home had never been properly upgraded, we had to replace all the plumbing, electrical, and mechanicals, which meant gutting the entire interior. There were also issues with the foundation, especially under one corner of the living room, which needed underpinning. Given the necessary excavation work, it made sense to enlarge the basement to better house the mechanicals and provide extra storage. This excavation also allowed us to lower the floor of the living room and, by raising the ceiling at the same time, we increased the room's height by eighteen inches. Along with new windows and French doors, we reshaped the proportions of the living room, making it substantially brighter and giving our clients a space that feels gracious and intimate.

During the time the house was "deboned, skinned, and gutted," as the husband likes to say, we installed radiant heating throughout, central air-conditioning, and a separate dehumidification system, taking pains to conceal the vents within the plaster cornices of every room. While the new interiors appear as they might have looked a century or more ago, all of the systems have been thoroughly modernized.

Left: Due to years of water penetration and rot, one corner of the living room needed to be excavated and underpinned, which gave us an opportunity to dig out the basement and lower the floors of the living room and library. In combination with raising the ceiling, the room became eighteen inches taller. These new proportions, new windows and new openings for French doors make it a gracious, lovely room that now opens directly onto an expansive terrace on the north and library on the east. Parquet de Versailles floors from reclaimed oak, a period mantel and plaster moldings complete the room. Radiant heating, central air-conditioning, and dehumidification systems were added throughout, although they were kept almost entirely invisible.

Above: We extended the footprint of the library with a box bay of full-height glass. The ceiling was raised and a generous plaster cove added. A new fireplace was built opposite the main seating group. The mirror above the mantel conceals a TV.

Opposite: The library's new windows look onto the south lawn and reveal the house's L-shape. The French oak moldings, paneling, and bookshelves are all new. We designed concealed motorized shades, in lieu of curtains.

Right: My initial sketch.

LIBRARY

Because of the house's proximity to the ocean, there is a consistent and lovely breeze off the water; the family can go weeks without using the air-conditioning. While the couple both prefer natural ventilation, they realized during the planning of the house that they disagreed on the matter of screens. The husband considered them ugly magnets for dirt and debris and didn't want to use them, but the wife couldn't imagine living in a house with unscreened, open windows. As a compromise we designed pocketing door and window screens that slide into the walls, out of sight when not in use. When in use they always look pristine because they remain protected during bad weather.

Working with David Easton, and especially Emilie Price from his office, the interior decor reflects the clients' aesthetic and sensibilities. Staying within a refined French country vocabulary, we detailed the interior with a blend of painted dado walls in the living room, dining room and entry, while in the library we installed full-height European oak paneling. Plaster crowns and parquet de Versailles floors on the ground level support this style. In the entry hall, through the central axis of the house, and out to the back terrace, we laid reclaimed limestone pavers that give the space a strong texture and age, connecting indoors to outdoors with a look that is spare and clean. Fireplaces are always a focus of period-inspired rooms; we used antique mantels in the living room with a beautiful antique mirror above, and a simpler limestone mantel in the dining room. In the oak-paneled library, which also serves as family room and office, a television is hidden behind the mirror above the simple limestone mantel.

In large pre-war houses, the room that almost always requires a complete rethink is the kitchen, and this one was no exception. In today's homes, family and friends congregate in the kitchen, but in the past, they were staff-centered; family rarely ventured into them. Here the original space was small and shut off from the rest of the house except for a double-acting door to the pantry and two small windows. We opened the walls between the kitchen and the breakfast porch so the larger area more easily accommodates the family and their guests. We lined the breakfast porch with French doors that, again, offer that incredible water view and let the breeze in, opening onto the rear patio. As for the kitchen itself, it is both highly functional, outfitted with the latest equipment, and warm and inviting. An adjacent hallway was transformed into a butler's pantry/bar that supports formal dining and informal entertaining.

To access the second floor, we installed a new oak stair with a closed stringer and carved oak balusters. We reconfigured many of the rooms on this floor so that each bedroom has two exposures and an en-suite bathroom; I think some of the most pleasing aspects of any room are multiple views especially with the sound of surf in the distance. While we stayed with a vocabulary similar to the first floor, we wanted to signal that this level was more private. Instead of the parquet de Versailles used on the first floor, here we used six-inch-wide oak plank flooring. We gave the doorways a slight barrel vault to soften its edges and provide a sense of intimacy. There's a master bedroom suite with a sitting room, bath and dressing room; the daughter's room; a master guest suite with a fireplace and generous window seat; and two other smaller guest rooms off the back stair and tucked into the roof, so they feel very sheltered. On the third floor, we designed a playroom and workout space.

Several steps from the Main House was the pool and Poolhouse, an undistinguished 1960s addition to the property that didn't relate to any other structures. We removed it, preserving the building's footprint, and designed a new brick-and-timber pavilion with a covered porch in the style of the Main House. The pool was refurbished and a hidden motorized cover added. Our clients and their guests can now sit in the cool shade under the eaves of the porch or they can retreat inside to enjoy the Poolhouse living room. In this space, we added dormer windows, front and back to function as a clerestory, making the space quite luminous. Our design includes a service kitchen/bar, cabana, bathrooms, outdoor showers, and a fireplace for year-round use.

Above: The new Poolhouse is a small brick pavilion embellished with a half-timbered covered porch, slender dormers, twin brick chimneys, and a swept roofline, all of which continue the aesthetic of the Main House.

Transforming the property's Gatehouse into a Tennis House was thoroughly enjoyable. Like all the buildings on the property, it had long been forlorn. This little jewel was originally the Caretaker's Lodge, so it had its own kitchen, dining area, bedroom and bathroom, all at a slightly reduced scale. When the owners said they wanted to add a tennis court — they're players and fans of the game — we chose to place it near the Gatehouse so the tiny building can be a staging space for outdoor entertaining around the court.

A tennis court is a significant design element, with a large footprint usually surrounded by a ten-foot fence. As much as tennis players love the game, most people think a tennis court does not add beauty to a well-designed landscape. The solution was to sink the court into the ground by five feet, which left five feet above ground that became hedge-fronted mesh at the service ends. We left the center areas open and built terraced seating.

Opposite: Hedges start to conceal a sunken tennis court with a seating area and steps that serve as modest bleachers.

Following page: The Guesthouse, built in the 1960s, was also in need of repair and replanning. We kept the basic structure, but designed an extensive renovation that altered the roof, enlarged the windows and added a timber porch that relates to the Main House and Poolhouse. We also worked with the landscape designer Deborah Nevins on a new cottage garden. Most importantly, we connected the Guesthouse to the Main House with an enclosed, skylit extension of the mudroom.

The Guesthouse, adjacent but not previously connected to the Main House, was also in pretty dire shape when our clients bought the property. Even though it was built in the 1960s, it needed a complete renovation. As its architecture wasn't particularly distinguished, we started by reworking the exterior, altering the roof and dormers, enlarging the windows on the first floor, adding a timber porch that relates to the Main House, and designing a private garden terrace. A fanciful addition in the front stairway was a bulls-eye window — an oeil-de-boeuf.

The interior was also completely reworked — a fully functioning kitchen opens to a new dining area and a new larger sitting room. A skylit connection to the Main House mud room was built to complete the plan. My clients wanted the Guesthouse redesigned so that friends, when they stayed, would have their own space and privacy. I can't think of a more thoughtful way to enjoy an extended visit.

From a site planning standpoint, the Guesthouse is the third "leg" of the enclosure of a new service court. When working on our projects, I am always looking for the best way to hide parked cars and service trucks — there always seem to be more than you would expect. For me, there is nothing less visually appealing than seeing the driveway of a beautiful house full of vehicles. The brick walls that surround the court are part of the structures and part of the garden wall. Adorned with vines and climbing roses, they transform the service court into a garden-like setting.

Working with landscape architect Deborah Nevins, the gardens near the house were re-organized and planted to appear as if they had always been a part of the original landscape.

In looking back, I have come to appreciate the client's patient approach to the phasing of the projects. Each building was renovated or added to in a thoughtful sequence. We spent nearly a decade renovating and upgrading this property, due to both the complications of construction and periods of "non-construction" when our clients simply wanted to enjoy their home. The couple adores it, and apparently, their friends do as well. They told me it's typical for neighbors to drop by for a morning coffee and stay for dinner; no one wants to leave. That is something I love hearing when our work is done.

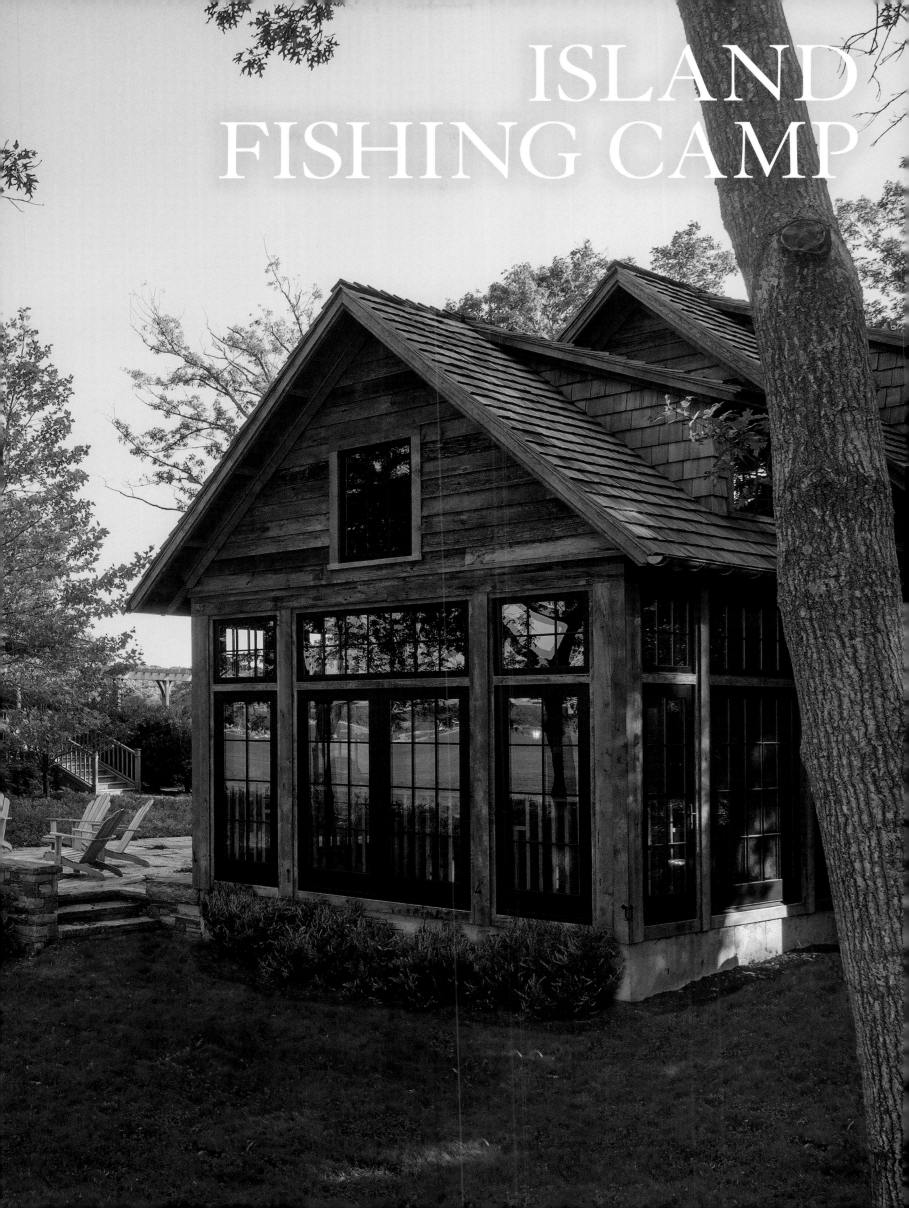

ISLAND FISHING CAMP

Above: Aerial views of an unusually preserved peninsula. When our clients were shown a 1960s–era ranch house and garage on this secluded property, they understood what a rare opportunity it presented.

Right: The cross-axial gable of the living room and running dormer of new second floor, with pool terrace in foreground.

A family of outdoor enthusiasts who had long adored spending summers on this island acquired an extraordinary wooded property, situated on the tip of a peninsula, where they hoped to create a three-season retreat. A tired '60s–era ranch house and garage surrounded by conserved woodland greeted us when we first arrived there for an inspection.

Standing on the site, the bay looks more like a great lake than an inlet of the Atlantic Ocean, as it is bounded by woods on all sides. That's in part what gave us the idea of designing an Adirondack-inspired fishing camp, reminiscent of those built in the late nineteenth- and early twentieth-centuries. To comply with the town's stringent land use restrictions and setback rules, we were required to maintain most of the footprint and portions of the existing structures, which were not especially well built, architecturally interesting or significant. We could only expand the footprint in a few areas. But, thankfully, we could add a second floor if we preserved the first-floor-wall-plate heights. Working within these very strict guidelines we devised an up-to-date modern retreat that references an earlier time.

One of our most dramatic interventions in the Main House was to raise and rotate the central roof to make a large cross-axial, gabled space with the long views to the north and south. We left the original low ceilings in the adjacent rooms so that one enters through a fairly compressed space. There is definitely an exhilarating moment when guests come into the main room with its double-height ceiling, two-story-high windows looking onto the bay, and great stone hearth. It's an expansive, light-filled room at the very center of the house.

On the first floor, the living room is flanked by low-ceilinged public areas (kitchen, entry hall, mudroom and breakfast room) on one side, and a series of private rooms (small study, powder room and large master suite) at the other. New bedrooms and baths were added above both. In these parts of the house, we were restricted to maintaining the same top-of-plate height. In the kitchen area, we increased the perceived ceiling height by removing the existing ceiling finishes and cladding the joists, gaining an extra ten inches of space and volume in between. That made the new kitchen and breakfast room much airier. We also radically replanned those rooms by joining them, switching the windows around to take better advantage of the views, designing oak cabinetry, and installing state-of-the-art appliances. We committed to using wood for all the walls, ceilings and floors to add texture and support the camp-like feeling.

Above: An early study of the exterior shows the addition of a second floor with new running dormers, new porches and chimney. The metal roof envisioned here developed into a cedar-shake roof.

Next pages: The new two-story living room opens to north and south with water views. Oak planking was used for floors, walls and ceiling throughout.

LIVING ROOM

Opposite: If there was a single architectural gesture that defined this project, it was the creation of a double-height living room. To enter this voluminous space, with its dramatic views to the water, the rustic gabled, timbered ceiling and massive stone hearth, is to feel far removed from urban pressures.

Above: The new fieldstone fireplace and chimney anchor the room and define a generous hearth for gathering of family and guests.

Left: My initial sketch.

RENEWING TRADITION

These pages: We increased the perceived ceiling height in this portion of the house by removing the existing ceilings and framing, then installing new exposed beams. In the kitchen and bar we designed oak cabinetry that received a color wash stain. A built-in banquette creates an informal eating area. We added state-of-the-art appliances, as well as a central island for sitting, talking and prepping food — all with multiple views to the porch and water beyond.

Above: A freestanding enameled steel bathtub is framed by a square, oversized window in the angled bay of the master bath, with full water views.

Right: The powder room, with its stone floor, also serves as a changing room as it opens onto the porch nearest the pool.

The main master suite is on the first floor, where I often recommend including a generous guest suite that can eventually become the master bedroom. Double French doors lead to a small private terrace.

With constraints on extending the building's footprint, we tried to be creative wherever we could within the available space. In the living room hallway, we designed a powder room that doubles as a full bath and a changing room for the pool, which is just outside, beyond the porch.

As a three-season vacation home, connection to the outdoors is quite important. We designed wrap-around porches outside the kitchen on the north and west sides of the house, and to the south off the main room for easy and protected connection to the outdoors. These generous exterior living spaces speak of the days before air-conditioning, when sitting in the shade of the porch with breezes from the water was the best way to stay cool on a hot summer day. The discreet addition of hidden, motorized insect screens make the south porch comfortable well into the evenings.

Above: The master bedroom is conveniently located on the ground floor, with access to the exterior.

Following pages: In the second-floor sitting/media room, the owners' collection of nautical flags complements the water view.

Previous page: The upstairs sitting/media room connects to one of two large guest suites and a bunk room to host extended family and friends.

Opposite: While the guest rooms are meant to look a bit rustic, they all feature en-suite baths and private balconies with views of the water.

Above: The indoor-outdoor connection extends into the window-lined second-floor bathroom; even the shower has a view.

Above: The Boathouse and the reconfigured Main House with new wrap-around porch are connected by a fire pit and outdoor seating area.

Right: An early sketch of the Boathouse, as seen from the water.

Opposite: The Main House and the Boathouse form a protected courtyard.

Once we had completed the design of the main house we focused our attention on transforming the garage, preserving the footprint as required. We designed a multi-purpose outbuilding containing a game room, guest suite and boat storage that resembles a weathered old boathouse that could have been original to the property. A new full basement included a hydraulic lift that provided access for additional car and additional boat storage.

We used reclaimed barn materials to create the feel of a late-1800s utility structure. The team searched for old reclaimed studs without a lot of nail holes on both sides, as we wanted it to appear as if the wall planks were the exterior sheathing nailed from the outside. These exposed stud walls, roughly hewn rafters and rescued floor planks from a threshing barn, create an authentic feel. Although an original boathouse would not have been insulated, here the roof is not only finished but completely insulated, as are the walls — allowing year-round use. Beneath those rugged floor planks is an advanced radiant-heating system. The boathouse may look rustic, but it's a refined rustic.

Situated this close to the ocean, these newly rebuilt structures now meet all hurricane codes, with new windows and doors to resemble carpenter-built windows — only much sturdier. Steel tie-downs and structural connections are hidden in the timberwork.

The real achievement of this property is the creation of a modern retreat that authentically recalls a simpler time.

Opposite: In place of the former garage we built a new boathouse that contains a game room, bar and pool table on the main floor, as well as boat storage below and a guest suite above. The exposed stud walls, roughly hewn rafters and rescued floor planks are meant to look unfinished.

Above: The game room can be opened on three sides, allowing it to function as an open-air pavilion in the summertime.

Left and above: The second floor of the boathouse includes a guest suite with a loft bedroom, sitting room and bathroom that has both a modern, glazed cube shower enclosure and old-fashioned toilet.

The owners, who did all the decorating, hung classic Hudson's Bay blankets instead of drapes on the partially-glazed loft doors. These doors can be swung open at the end of the season to allow boats and other equipment to be stored on the second floor.

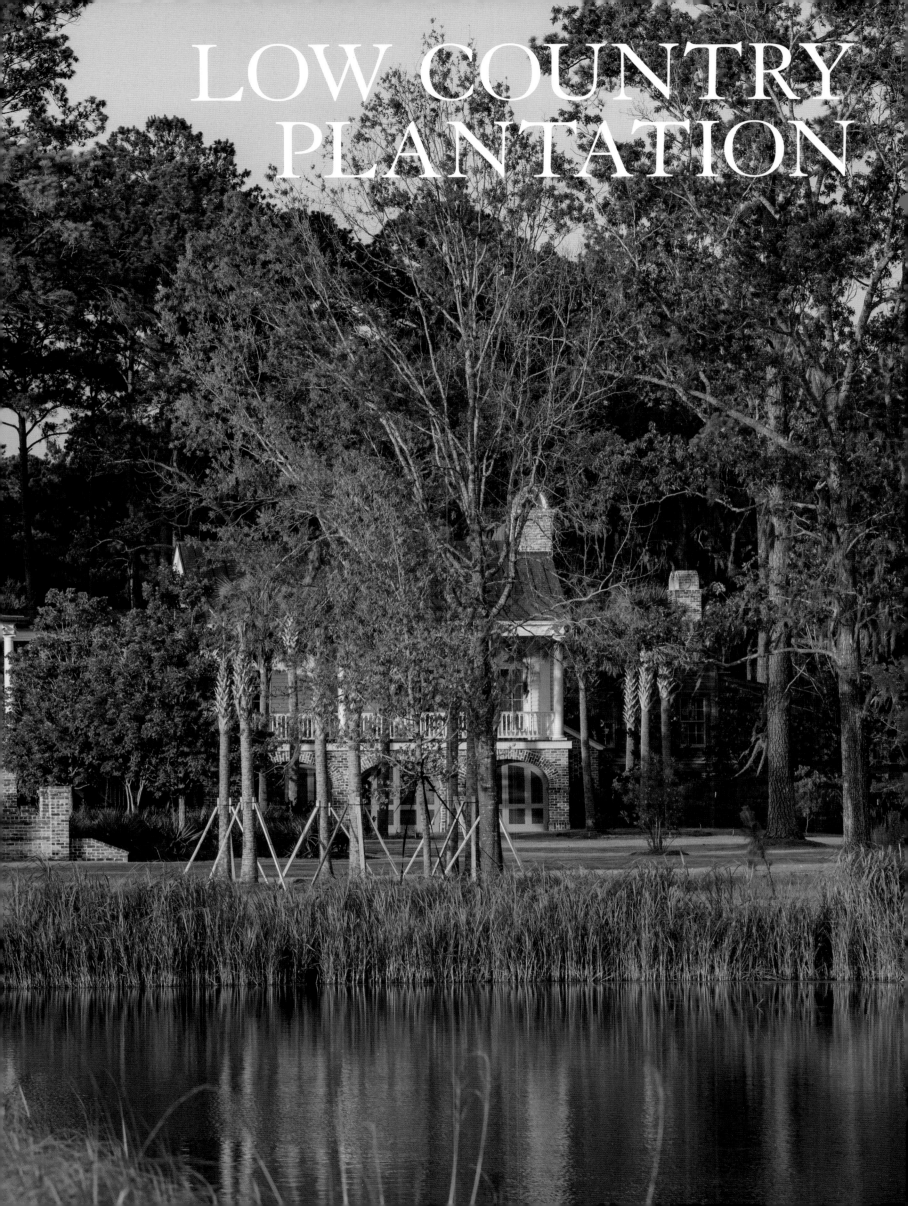

LOW COUNTRY PLANTATION

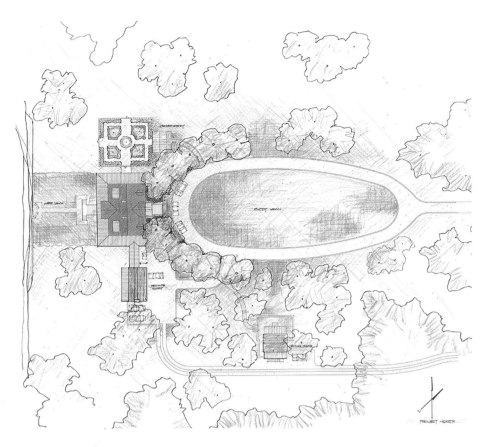

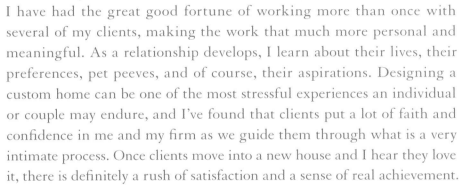

I have had the great good fortune of working more than once with several of my clients, making the work that much more personal and meaningful. As a relationship develops, I learn about their lives, their preferences, pet peeves, and of course, their aspirations. Designing a custom home can be one of the most stressful experiences an individual or couple may endure, and I've found that clients put a lot of faith and confidence in me and my firm as we guide them through what is a very intimate process. Once clients move into a new house and I hear they love it, there is definitely a rush of satisfaction and a sense of real achievement.

My relationship with the owners of this Low Country plantation preceded any design commissions, as the wife and my wife have known each other since they were girls. Their families spent summers at the same lakefront cottage community in northern Michigan, and our families have continued that tradition. This project is the most complex that I have undertaken for them, and for me it is the most special because not only is this their primary residence in their retirement years, but it also presented the chance to design a number of outbuildings, five in all, in the local vernacular of the Low Country. Our goal was to create a new family compound that would feel as if it has always been there.

Avid outdoors people, hunters, bird lovers and conservationists, the couple has strong ties to the South. As a child, the wife spent many happy summers visiting her grandmother in nearby Athens, Georgia; it is her dearest wish that one day her grandchildren enjoy similar vacations at her home.

Opposite: Aerial view of the plantation looking north east.

Upper left: My initial design for the site showed the Main House, located adjacent to the rice field and marsh grounds, with an historically inspired elliptical entry drive enclosing a lawn, the connected Guest House and nearby Cook House. To the north is the walled garden and conservatory and to the west is the main pasture garden, adjacent to a restored field.

Upper and middle right: The entry drive was laid out to circumnavigate an aged live oak — easily 200 years old. The drive the crosses a cow pasture to a pair of gates and cattle guard.

Bottom right: Aerial view looking west and south west.

Next pages: Aerial view of the main house and surrounding structures and gardens.

Originally part of a larger antebellum rice plantation, the property had been used for the past century for hunting, logging, and farm life. We couldn't find any evidence of an original plantation house, but a simple single-story hunting "lodge" still existed from the 1920s, which is where the couple first lived when visiting the property during the early phases of construction. As much of the land had been used for rice farming, it still had traces of a network of dikes for channeling water from the Combahee River into the various rice fields. The dikes, although in disrepair, were in part what made the property so attractive to the husband. Once the land had been acquired, he began a program of restoration so that he could regulate the water's depth in various dikes and parts of the marshland, creating a more complex habitat to attract a greater variety of birds. Different types of birds feed in different depths of water, hence the various lengths of their beaks and legs. (Another fortunate aspect of my work: the chance for lifelong learning, particularly when working in diverse places for clients who have a broad variety of interests.)

Just as the couple reclaimed the ancient dikes for contemporary conservation, they sought to use the Low Country's historical architectural vocabulary, adapting it for today's living.

The Main House demonstrates how beautifully the local architecture's characteristic elements still respond to this specific geography and climate. We situated the house at the edge of a field amid ancient live oaks and pine trees, overlooking both the restored dikes and a wide expanse of water and sky. Being close to the water, this southwest-facing location promised beautiful sunsets and also the advantage of gentle breezes. It also meant the first floor had to be elevated more than eight feet above the ground to meet local regulations based on hurricane storm surges. We took inspiration from some of the area's earliest homes and built a foundation of raised brick arches. This approach endowed the home with elegance and solidity, while at the same time allowing any floodwaters to pass underneath. (In fact, the house survived hurricanes Irma and Matthew without damage.) Moreover, as the fields and marshes are populated with snakes (some poisonous) and alligators, an elevated house helps to keep the critters outside. The arches also allow air to flow underneath the house for cooling during the long hot, humid summers.

ERIC J. SMITH ARCHITECT P.C.   FEBRUARY 13, 2013

Main House

We located the Main House at the edge of the fields, with wide views of the live oaks, pines, water, and sky. All of the buildings reflect our extensive research on Low Country architectural traditions. Here design features include deep porches along the front and back facades, exterior staircases to the first floor, and high brick arches to protect the house in hurricane or flood conditions. Brick walls, a clay tile roof and divided-light windows were chosen for their durability and historic character.

Opposite: The entry sequence begins on the front porch and proceeds into the entry/stair hall. A half-glass door and side lights, in combination with a fan light, provide ample daylight to the space.

Above left: The axial entry sequence continues from the stair hall through the library, onto the rear porch, releasing to a view of a restored rice field.

Above right: Cross axial view to living room from entry hall.

Left: My original sketch of the entry, looking to the library on axis with the entry door.

ENTRY

These pages: Our approach to the interior architecture reflects the historic homes of Beaufort and Charleston. Working again with the client's interior designer Diana Hambleton, the furniture and color palette of the living room are in harmony with the architecture. Our clients particularly enjoy the living room with its three exposures and access to porches front and back. A large bay window and fireplace with an antique wood mantel organize the seating arrangements. As there is no formal dining room in the Main House, the English drop-leaf table can seat six for intimate dining.

These pages and following pages: The library — which connects the entry hall, living room, kitchen, and west porch — is the crossroads and heart of the house. In the living room, an antique mantel and over-mantel were procured from a dealer in Philadelphia. Reclaimed southern pine was used for all the woodwork and bookcases, handscraped and finished to complement the mantel.

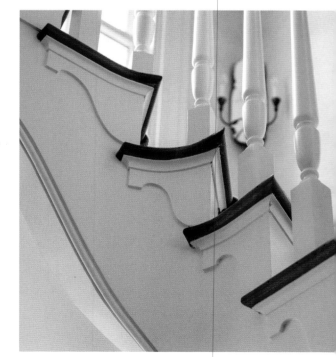

Left: A wood-burning brick hearth is the focal point of the kitchen, and features a niche underneath for log storage. The woven pendant lamp is an example of the Low Country's great tradition of basket-weaving, still practiced today.

Top: The breakfast area viewed from the hearth across the kitchen was designed to read as a "glassed-in" portico of the wrap-around main porch.

Above: My original sketch of the kitchen.

Having previously worked very closely with the couple's longtime decorator, Diana Hambleton (whose nearby house I also designed), we knew their tastes, preferences and the style they enjoy in interior design. Diana's choice of hand-painted wallpaper in the entry foyer and the soft tones of the living room perfectly complement the architectural details in the staircase and proportions of the living room. One of the most used spaces in the Main House is the library, which connects to the entry, living room, kitchen and porch. The pine-paneled room's floor-to-ceiling bay window is on axis with the front door, opening out to showcase the property yet still allow for "nesting" time in a traditionally furnished, book-lined library with a fireplace. It is truly the heart of the home.

The focal point of the kitchen is its large wood-fired hearth, designed with a traditional brick quoin surround. The owners tend to enjoy informal meals in the house, which happen either at a rattan table on the breakfast porch, or at the island in the kitchen. For small groups there is a drop-leaf table in the living room that seats six. Just as often, the couple enjoys eating comfortably by the fire in the library just off the kitchen.

Opposite: The bar hall is just off the main stair, serving as a link to the mudroom and breakfast porch beyond.

Above: The wine cellar, in the Guesthouse.

Opposite: The winding staircase in the Main House features turned balusters and a hand-crafted classic volute banister. We designed a corbel detail into the staircase based on the wave motif often seen in sea captains' homes, appropriate for the region.

Opposite: The second-floor master suite faces south with three exposures and is flooded with daylight, offering expansive views of the property, especially from its walk-out porch.

Above: The butternut-lined master bath features a vintage tub and pedestal sink, suggesting that this room was adapted from a prior use.

Below: My original sketch for the master bedroom.

RENEWING TRADITION

Left: Porches have been an important component of virtually every type of house in the southern United States since the eighteenth century. The deep porches of the Main House act as outdoor living rooms, offering shade and breezes in hot weather, views to the gardens, fields and marshes. A ceiling fan helps keep the bugs at bay.

RENEWING TRADITION

Guesthouse

One of the best ways to keep guests and hosts happy is to make sure everyone has enough space to be together and to be apart. The guest wing is a separate building connected to the Main House by this breezeway porch. The inset stair and balustrade design are historically inspired.

To my mind, the homes best suited for hosting extended family are ones that also let everyone have their own space. In full agreement, the husband suggested we plan a generous guest suite, but not in the Main House; rather in a wing attached to it by a covered, open-air porch. As much as he and his wife enjoy their children and grandchildren, they also relish their peace and quiet. Knowing how much they desired tranquility in the Main House, I added vestibules with sliding doors outside the master bedroom to further insulate their rooms from the patter of high-spirited children. These little architectural pauses have another benefit: they provide convenient spots for concealed storage, mechanical controls and dimmers, all hidden out of sight.

These pages: The Guesthouse is built for privacy. Separated by a covered walkway from the Main House, it features a generous bedroom with windows on three sides, plus a private walk-out porch. The antique, early-American pine mantel is surrounded by a hand-painted English tiled slip.

Gardens

Left: With the main garden, the husband, an accomplished gardener, realized the walled garden he had always wanted. Adjacent to the Main House and visible from the living room and porches, the garden is enclosed by a brick wall, in contrast to the larger property with its hundreds of acres of marshland and wild wooded growth.

Top: Collaborating with local landscape architect Sheila Wertimer, we devised a formal plan, including a vine-covered arbor, garden shed and English conservatory. A small orchard beyond anchors an agricultural use, and the garden's plantings include herbs and vegetables, which winter over in the conservatory.

Above: Sheila designed the main lawn as a raised parterre, creating a formal space as a transition to the native grasses beyond.

Cook House

There is intentionally no formal dining room in the Main House. Rather, my clients envisioned a separate building, the Cook House, where they would entertain.

Opposite: The dining room is supported by a small prep kitchen. The large fireplace evokes a cooking hearth from an earlier time.

As noted earlier, while there are several areas in the Main House for casual dining, the couple requested we forgo a formal dining room and instead design a "Cook House," a small, separate outbuilding nearby. For occasions when they entertain on a larger scale, they have drinks with guests in the living room or on the porch before walking down a winding gravel path through beautifully landscaped grounds to the Cook House. With the capacity to seat up to fourteen guests, the Cook House is modeled on the summer kitchen, a building type that was once quite common along the eastern seaboard that separated the functions and risk of fire from the Main House.

Up the steps there's a small porch from which everyone enters the dining room with its generous hearth and expansive table. Knowing that the room would be used often in winter, we designed it to be especially appealing in candlelight.

Pool and Poolhouse

The pool and Poolhouse were the first things we designed, so that the couple and their visiting children could have a place to relax as the rest of the projects were under way. Accessed by an azalea-lined lane — an early drive — the pool site is very private, bordered by live oaks and pecan trees.

Above: Because the Poolhouse is so far from the Main House, its kitchen is fully functional, including a full complement of appliances to support entertaining.

Right: The Poolhouse was inspired by an old carriage house, with a wide-arched central walkway, shingle roof, pergola, Gothic picket fence and trellises. An adjacent brick pump house muffles noise from the pool equipment.

Game House

The Game House, sitting on a slight rise, needed to be raised only a few steps to meet code relative to flood level.

The building is clad in sinker cypress clapboard and trim that we allowed to age naturally. The windows are hurricane rated and the shutters are fully functioning, so they can be closed during storms and off season.

285

Previous pages and these pages: The name is a bit of a double entendre: the Game House does feature a billiard table, board games and other amusements, but it has another role as well. As outdoors-people and hunters, my clients wanted a place where shooting parties could gather before dawn to dress and prepare for the day's hunt. Upon their return, they can deposit their equipment before enjoying a beverage by the fire or on the back porch overlooking the water and savoring the sunset.

With its rustic, natural cypress facade, working shutters and bishops' cap chimneys (a traditional Low Country feature that prevents rain from going down the chimney), the Game House serves many functions. Part entertainment space, part hunting support, part office for the husband, it also has an exercise room. The hub for activities before and at the end of every hunting outing, the Game House is where the group meets to pick up or drop off their equipment and gear. After dinner or on a non-hunting afternoon, family and guests can meet here to enjoy its large sitting room, bar, pool table, TV, raised fireplace, and sunsets on the rear porch.

Ice House

Above and right: The small but hardworking Ice House doubles as a larder for the entire property, with a walk-in refrigerator and freezer. Another room is outfitted to clean and flash-freeze birds or game from their hunting forays, allowing guests to take home quail, duck, et cetera.

The Ice House, situated adjacent to the Game House, has a work area for cleaning birds and game that, once dressed, can be flash-frozen so guests can take them home after their visit. It also functions as a larder, with a commercial-grade walk-in refrigerator and freezer, an essential feature for this remote property.

Horse Barn

The extended roofs on either side of this classic timber barn create loafing sheds, which provide shaded areas to wash down horses after an outing.

In the past, a mule cart would have been used to transport the shooting party to the location of the day's shoot; today, electric ATVs suffice.

Top: We designed this office for the plantation manager, who watches over the property, family and guests 365 days a year, no small task.

Above: A bespoke horse stall.

Right: While years ago the barn would have housed mules and their wagons, this one shelters horses, with supporting spaces for tack and feed. Details include a handsome brick floor and shepherd's crook sconces.

The horse barn includes spaces for tack and feed, as well as an office for the plantation manager. To achieve the feel that the barn dated to the nineteenth century, we called upon the same timberwrights from Vermont who had worked on the Game House. A significant challenge was to engineer the structure to meet the hurricane codes and conceal all of the necessary steel connections, preserving the look of a true timber frame. The timbers were cut, adzed, hewn, fit and pre-assembled in North Springfield, Vermont, then disassembled, labeled, numbered, and shipped 950 miles away to the site, where they were re-assembled by the same team. The barn is the result of a great deal of effort, which successfully creates the sense of age, handwork and custom joinery we were seeking.

My hope is that, as a result of the attention we paid to the siting, materials, style and detailing of each building, guests arriving today will assume that all of these structures have been here for many years, maybe a century or more. This historically informed, modern compound, conceived for a twenty-first-century couple and their family and friends, treats all who visit to a remarkable Low Country experience.

Acknowledgments

"Ah to build to build, that is the noblest art of all the arts...." This passage from Longfellow is no less inspiring to me now than when I began my career.

When I set out to write this book it was to commemorate the 30th anniversary of my practice. As a way to share this milestone, I had planned to just pull together some photographs and reflections that I thought family, friends and clients would find interesting. I soon found that reviewing and evaluating 30 years of work was both daunting and extraordinarily humbling, and that creating a meaningful expression was more than I could do on my own. Creating a monograph is far more like building a book than merely writing one; and as with a custom home, one needs skilled professionals to guide the way. Thankfully I had Brad Collins and Group C, Iva Kravitz, and Will Cheung from my office to work with me in preparing and editing what quickly grew to be a more expansive and, I hope, more interesting collection of photographs, drawings, anecdotes and recollections. I thank each of them for their care, patience and thoughtfulness in helping me craft this book. I am also grateful to Douglas Curran of Rizzoli for choosing to publish it — an exciting realization of all of our effort. I would also like to thank Marisa Bartolucci for her generous Introduction, and Alexa Hampton for her kind words — and yes, we have no bananas!

As I looked back over these three decades of practice, it became clear that every project has been a journey, each different but somehow connected, each offering its own set of challenges and rewards, and that with each I have been fortunate to have been joined by so many dedicated, talented and supportive people — to all of you — thank you.

It has often been said that there can be no great project without a great client. It has been my good fortune to have worked with so many great clients — thoughtful, energetic and purposeful individuals who have challenged us to create something where there was nothing, and who have embraced the results with enthusiasm and gratitude. Their willingness to trust us on this journey, and to be guided in the realization of a shared vision, has allowed me the opportunity to work on projects and in places that I would have never imagined as a young architect. Especially rewarding has been the chance to work with some of our clients multiple times — it has been an honor and a pleasure. It has also been extremely satisfying to create a number of legacy homes and to then witness them being comfortably enjoyed by several generations at the same time — just as had been planned. But what I find to be most gratifying is to hear how, years later, these homes still fulfill the needs and desires of our clients — how they still enjoy living in them. To each of our clients I offer my sincere thanks.

As to the process of building one of these homes, I often share with my staff that for me, architecture does not exist unless it gets built. A nice design and a beautiful set of drawings, unless it is constructed, is just that — a "nice" design. Transforming our drawings into homes has been the work of literally thousands of skilled, dedicated and talented builders, contractors, craftsman, suppliers, fabricators and so many others. On reflection, it is fair say that we have learned from each other and, from my perspective, all of our collaborations have been enjoyable and rewarding. Together we have created homes that have exceeded everyone's expectations.

It's the *quality* of the energy of the building team that manifests itself into the quality of the homes that our clients will experience every day. The care taken to survey the site properly; to frame the spaces carefully; to anticipate both the interior and exterior finishes; to integrate all the systems within this skeleton without compromising the aesthetic; to apply every finish with the highest quality and integrity; and to make every edge, corner and surface as perfect as possible — this all contributes to creating beautiful and in many cases remarkable homes, built to survive the effects of time, weather and use, and to feel as if they have always been there.

Of course, getting from initial design discussions and early freehand sketches to a set of construction drawings is no less challenging than the building process. It takes endless hours of effort by each member of the design team, the core of which are the dedicated architects, drafters, designers and support staff that have been part of my practice for these many years. I have been extremely fortunate to have a top-quality staff, some who have stayed with our firm for 20 years or more. I thank you each for your time, talents and energy — the projects included in this book (and not) are a testimony to your efforts. I am also especially thankful to the group of fellow professionals with whom we have collaborated — the interior designers and decorators, engineers, landscape architects and the myriad of project-specific consultants who have contributed their expertise.

When I started this book, I also thought that I might come across the one startlingly clear moment that I could identify as the beginning of my career. I soon realized that there was no one point; rather, there were any number of people and moments along the way, each a new starting point, each a new trail head. Whether it was my early interest in photography or crossing paths with a remarkable high school teacher, facing the choice between changing universities or changing majors as a college freshmen, a transformational year studying abroad or even the unfortunate accident of a broken light bulb and the resulting fire that led me to a Lake Forest renovation and in turn on to New York City, the path has been full of unexpected turns, ridges and troughs, retreats and false starts. It has also been a path crowded with fascinating people. Certainly one was David Easton, who offered me the chance to step onto the moving train that was his design office and to thrive in the roll of engineer, ticket taker and conductor. Collaborating with David during the first portion of my career was an extraordinary experience. Those early projects allowed me to develop as an architect, to refine my design skills and technical abilities, and to form my practice. Even as my practice expanded and I began to collaborate with others, David and I still occasionally collaborated. Those experiences remain a warm memory.

While everyone that I have included above, whether mentioned by name or not, has contributed to the creation of not only this book but to my career and practice, none has contributed more than my family. I thank my parents, Roland and Dody, who were, and are, understanding and patient, for starting me off on this adventure with a firm footing. But truly none of this would have been possible without the love and support of my wife Elasah and our children Heather and Baxter. This profession is not of the 9–5 variety; the long hours and countless evenings and weekends working over my drawing board, in meetings or traveling to sites, was all time spent away from them. Words cannot replace this nor compensate for the extra efforts that fell to Elasah. I am forever grateful to have had the chance to pursue these dreams with your understanding and help — it is to you that I dedicate this book.

Staff

1987 — Now

Dario Agarabi	Kamil Hattoum	Amanda Norman
Ricardo Arosemena	Andrew Hayes	Susan O'Brien
Martina Bacarella	Kassandra Hazlehurst	Mary Ortega
Morgan Bartholick	Amanda Hernandez	Lavinia Pana
Khalil Benanni	Jamison Heyliger	John Parker
Nebojsa Berjan	Masayo Hirano	Anthony Pellino
Alejandra Blanco	Marc Hochman	Emily Perez del Puerto
Andres Blanco	Amanda Holenstein	Pavlo Piddoubny
Bogdan Borgovan	Timothy Hook	Lisa Procida
William Brockschmidt	Ryan Hughes	Sean Rasmussen
Kennith Bryant	Igor Idak	Amy Raymond
Tiffany Burke	Brian Jackson	Kimberly Rispanti
Lisa Cancel	Jessica Jain	Sara Anne Rockwell
Lyn Carrick	Chris Jeffcoat	Morgan Rolontz
Louis Cespedes	Dieynaba Johnson	Susan Salsbury
Skye Chapman	Jill Kapadia	Joel Santos
Elena Chaykovskaya	Sara Kastner	Richard Sammons
Ji Yeon Choe	Margaret Keller	Kanna Sato-Chioldi
William Cheung	Heather Kelsey	Benjamin Sirota
Ashley Cisneros	Arthur Kipel	Trisha Snyder
Allison Cooper	Jaqueline Knoch	Matthew Standeven
Rachael Corcia	Michael Kudler	Kateri Stewart
Christina Corralez	Michael Lambdin	Benjamin Sutton
Megan Czaja	Jeffrie Lane	Zaharenia Svingos
Ron Czajka	Susan Law	Peter Talty
Nadine Dacanay	Mary Linehan	Siu Tam
Kristina Deluca	Andrea Lofgren	Manuel Tan
Kenneth Dietz	Carole Logie	Giovanna Taylor
Crystal Dixon	Diana Lopez	James Thompson
Kim Doggett	Charles Macbride	Andrzej Tobiasz
Johnny Donadic	Rachel Mallard	Dominick Tubito
Erik Dorsett	Heather Mangrum	Charisse Turner
Dori Eisenhauer	Dino Marcantonio	Kirsten Van Aalst
Tod Elliot	Nora Martin	Bernard Vauzanges
Robert Epley	Adrian Mathe	Frank Visconti
Nadia Fante	Trina McKinney	Jeff Vollmer
Andrew Friedman	Rachel Mesagna	Omar Walker
Cristiana Gallo	Vladimir Minakov	Lily Wang
Petra Garza	Philipp Mohr	Edward Watkins
Julio Gavilanes	Sally Morales	Ed Wendt
Jennifer Gomez	Christopher Moran	Myriam Yee
Monica Grancaric	Campbell Morrison	Ken Yost
Renia Hamlett	Silvia Neri	Ron Youngblood
Yoshiko Pia Hasegawa	Elaine Newman	Nicole Zielinski

Photography Credits

Brittany Ambridge
Forward

George Cott
Florida Riverfront, all photographs

Mike Kelley
Front Endsheet, p. 125, Low Country Plantation, all photographs

Nathan Kirkman
Lakefront Beaux-Arts, all photographs, p. 124
Stone Manse Updated, all photographs

Eric Laignel
P. 9, Art Collector's Pied-à-Terre, all photographs

David Duncan Livingston
California Georgian, p. 26(top), 34(bottom), 35, 36, 38-39, 40-41,
45(bottom right), 46(bottom left)

Peter Margonelli
California Georgian, p. 22, 24, 26(bottom left), 28-30, 32, 34(top),
42, 44, 45(top & bottom left), 47-48
Dutch Colonial on the Sound, p. 64, 67(left), 68-73, 76-77, 79-80, 86-89
Queen Anne Revived, p. 10, 114(top), 116(top), 117(top & bottom left),
118(top), 119(top), 120-121
Hamptons French Country, p. 194, 197, 202-203, 210-213
Island Fishing Camp, p. 214-216, 218-222, 224-227, 228(top), 229-231,
233(bottom right), 234-239

Steven Mays
Hamptons French Country, p. 2, 190-192, 196, 198-201, 204-209, Back Endsheet
Dutch Colonial on the Sound, p. 4

John McManus
Carolina Guest House, all photographs

Sargent Photography
Dutch Colonial on the Sound, p. 60, 66, 74, 78, 82-85

All other images courtesy of Eric J Smith Architect.
Every effort has been made to contact the holders of copyrighted material.
Omissions will be corrected in future editions if the publisher is notified in writing.